Liquorice All-Sorts

A GIRL GROWING UP

by

Muriel Breen

MOYTURA PRESS

DUBLIN

This book was typeset by
Gilbert Gough Typesetting Ltd for
Moytura Press, 4 Arran Quay, Dublin 7.

A catalogue record for this book
is available from the British Library.

ISBN 1-871305-15-2

ACKNOWLEDGMENT

The publishers acknowledge the permission of
The Blackstaff Press to reproduce on page 79
Bangor, Spring 1916 by John Hewitt from
The Collected Poems of John Hewitt.

Printed in Ireland by
Colour Books Ltd, Dublin.

The author (right) photographed with her two sisters,
Nan (left) and Helen.

To my niece, Anne

My thanks to Mary Rose Callaghan for help and encouragement and to my grandniece, Charlotte, for deciphering my scribbles.

ACROSTIC FOR A LADY

born 31 December 1899

Midnight and my gay nineties were over.
Upon the stroke of twelve they fled away.
Ring them back in then, for the century
I entered at a loss in the beginning
Enters its nineties now, alive and sinning—
Like me in my *belle epoque*, still young as ever.

Seamus Heaney

They were extremely boring walks and one day, in a spirit of bravado, we purloined a halfpenny from the loose money on the kitchen sideboard and bought liquorice all-sorts from Mrs Murphy's sweet shop, two doors away. She gave us awfully good value and so, fortified, we set off for our walk. The difficulty, of course, was to eat the delicious sweets without being seen. . . .

I

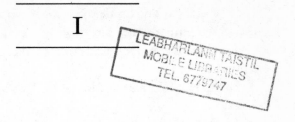

It was my birthday, 31st December 1903, and I was three.
My Daddy had said we'd have a little party just for four,
with a present and a cake. But for some reason he'd forgotten.

Everybody had.

I wasn't even allowed into Mummy's room and I was
miserable. My little sister, Nan, was playing with her dolls —
she was two and hadn't any sense. And she didn't care about
my birthday.

"It's my birthday," I shouted, running into the kitchen.

Bridget, our maid, was there, looking hot and cross. She
had let the fire out and couldn't get it lit again. In those days
everything was cooked on the big black range, so it was an
awful bother if it went out.

"It's my birthday," I reminded her.

Bridget furiously raked the dead coals. "Bother your
birthday!"

She didn't care either. Her hair was wild and her work
apron, which she wore over her blue and white striped dress,
was horridly smudged. The kitchen was horrid too, gloomy
and dark. I sat on the floor.

"Take care, or the cockroaches will get you," Bridget
warned furiously.

She was always talking about cockroaches. They were
great long creatures who came out at night, hundreds and
hundreds of them.

"Where do they come from?" I asked, peering at the floor.

But she was too busy to answer.

Then my Daddy came in. He was tall and handsome and
gay and I loved him more than anyone. His specs were

crooked that day and his tie too. I looked up hopefully. Surely he had remembered my birthday?

He picked me up, tossing me in the air. "Guess what's happened?"

Before I could answer, he said, "You've got a new baby sister!"

I wasn't impressed. I didn't want a baby sister for a birthday present.

"You'll have your birthday tomorrow with a real present and a cake. Your birthday on New Year's day for a change! Isn't that something to look forward to?"

It seemed a long, long time to wait but there was no choice. I wasn't even allowed to say goodnight to Mumper — we always called our mother that. I did vaguely wonder if she were sick or something. So, after a tea of bread, butter and jam, a disappointed little girl was put to bed by Bridget without much ceremony. Most probably I fought with my sister that night, as we tended to fight in bed. And most probably Bridget came in to stop us. I just can't remember. It's difficult to throw your mind back ninety years.

My parents had been married for at least three years before I appeared, and then my two sisters followed in quick succession — only three years to the day between me and my youngest sister. I was only fourteen months when Nan appeared. Who was to take care of me when my mother was fully occupied by the new baby? My father, of course. Our finances did not run to a real nursemaid. Of that, I'm sure. And I often think that my early acquaintance with my father was the reason for the special love between us.

Athough my parents weren't wealthy, there was always a Bridget in my childhood — when one left, another came. They were country girls who worked in the kitchen with my mother for a few shillings a week and were usually cross. But the next day, that particular Bridget was in much better form. In the afternoon she changed her apron — she always changed it in the afternoon — and dressed me in my best frock. I was to have my party at last. But I was surprised to hear that it was to be in Mumper's room. What sort of party was that?

I went in shyly. Inside a fire was burning in the grate and there were flowers on the table. Mumper was sitting on the sofa in her blue dressing gown with her frizzy fair hair on her shoulders like a little girl. Her hair was very, very curly and shoulder length. But it was usually pinned up with pins she left all over the house. Why not now?

Her arms were wide open. "Happy birthday, Muriel."

I flew into them. "Aren't you going to look at your little sister?" she said, after hugging me and sitting me down beside her.

I wasn't really interested, but went to look anyway. The tiny baby was all wrapped up in the cradle. She was sound asleep, just like any other baby, nothing to make a fuss of. Why didn't they get a boy for a change, I wondered? I already had a sister. Did I need two? Then Daddy arrived with Nan in his arms and plonked her down. Bridget followed, smiling for once and carrying a big tray with tea and lemonade and a wonderful birthday cake with three candles burning on it.

I could see a parcel under Daddy's arm. My present, I was sure. He gave me the parcel and I tore the wrapping off. It was a story book, a great big, shiny story book. My favourite thing.

I turned over page after page. It was full of pictures: the Sleeping Beauty, Cinderella, and lots and lots of others.

"We'll read one after we have our tea," Mumper said. "You can choose."

I chose the Babes in the Woods. As my mother read, I imagined the lost children, wandering hand and hand in that darkening, frightening forest. Then they lay down to rest and the birds came and covered them with leaves. Of course, they died, so I cried and cried. Tragedy had entered my life for the first time.

Perhaps this is why I remember my third birthday. The book was banished for ever after. I was given another one, of course. But the memory of the first book with its terrible story lingers on like a nightmare through all the years. That day is still as clear as yesterday. It was the real beginning of my life because it's the very first thing I remember. The contrast between the love and loveliness in that bedroom and the cruel fate of the children was printed indelibly on my heart. I was three years and one day old.

A happy childhood is something which remains with you. Mine has sustained me all my life. It began in Bangor, a little seaside town on the north east coast of our island. It was an Ireland which was very different to today. We were one country then, there were no cars poisoning the beautiful clean air and women wore long trailing skirts. As the sole survivor of my family, the last pebble on the beach, I can at least describe a small corner of it. I was born a few hours before the new century began. People have always commented on the date, but it was never important. I can't take any credit for an accident of birth. Anyway I've always found birthdays a bit of an anti-climax.

Even a hundred years ago Bangor was a commuter town. It is only twelve or fourteen miles from Belfast and those who could afford it travelled by train to the pure sea air away from the smoke and racket of the increasingly prosperous industrial city. So Bangor for the most part was residential. From about the fifth century onwards, it was one of the great seats of ancient Irish learning. Today an Abbey church stands on the remains of the beautiful old ruins of Bangor Abbey to remind us of past splendours, when the monks set forth to preach the Gospel. The church has no pews, just chairs. The Abbey is very important to the people of Bangor. It was important in my childhood too, as was religion. My father was ardently Church of Ireland, but as a child I was never aware of any differences in religion. Bangor was mainly Protestant but in those days there was no ill-feeling, as far as I could tell. The Roman Catholic population tended to live together in old

Bangor, but the different clergy mixed amicably.

My parents came to Bangor on their marriage and were literally strangers in a strange land. They had always lived in the country, which was very different to this small breezy town with its grey sea and stuck-up inhabitants. What they had to be stuck up about, my mother didn't know. They had no land, just bits of gardens and a church or two, a railway station and some shops in a long street. Like most Irish country people my mother had a deep love for the land. She liked broad green fields and meadows like the Tyrone countryside where she'd grown up with never a house in sight. Not little pokey gardens where you couldn't swing a cat. And then there was that awful sea always going in and out. I think she hated it at first. Oh, the Bangor people were friendly enough, she admitted, but distinctly not her kind. They didn't speak with her soft Tyrone accent, but with a harsh gutteral one. But Bangor was where we had to live, and that was that.

"Live old horse and you'll get grass," was what Dad always said. It didn't seem to make sense to me.

Our first Bangor house was cold and damp with long dreary passages and a funny smell — "That's them cock-roaches," Bridget had told me. Little tiny rivulets of water ran down the walls on wet days and sometimes mushrooms grew on the floor. It was a death trap and not fit for people to live in, let alone important people like us, my Dad said. But that was all to be changed. We were going to an absolutely new house as soon as it was ready. In the meantime, he and my mother tried to accustom themselves to their new environ-ment — as she said philosphically, you could get used to anything.

2

Looking back, I can't remember my father ever talking about his boyhood. His mother and father were never mentioned, so I have had to put together what little I know. Obviously he wasn't like Topsy who just growed.

The name Breen was originally O'Brien. My father came from the South, round Nenagh or somewhere in Tipperary, and was the younger of twins. His mother had died in childbirth and, a couple of years later, his father died too. There was an elder brother, and the three boys were passed from one lot of relatives to another — not a happy arrangement, and probably the reason he never talked about it. But they were all well educated and destined for professional careers of some sort. In those days, all of Ireland was administered by the British.

The elder brother, Willie, and George, my father's twin departed to South Africa, perhaps under the influence of the Boer War. My father, Joe, decided to stay in Ireland and joined the Civil Service. He opted for the Board of Works, because that entailed moving about from place to place and he would not be confined to an office.

He was posted to Belfast, the centre from which he was to travel in the Northern counties. He was lucky enough to find congenial digs or lodgings, with several other young men. I think they probably fancied themselves as gay young men about town and probably they were.

Most of his time was spent travelling in the country. There were recognised places to stay overnight and the lodgers participated in whatever local functions were taking place. A pleasant unattached young man was always welcome. It was at one of these affairs in Magherafelt, probably something to do with the local church, that Joe Breen met the youthful and lovely Elizabeth Booth.

It was love at first sight. Joe was knocked sideways by the lively, fair-haired girl and she stated on more than one occasion that her heart stopped beating. My mother was given to exaggeration, of course. But my father was very good-looking with smooth black hair and vivid blue eyes — a complete contrast to the country bumpkins she was accustomed to. Joe had no doubts at all. He was soon visiting Liz at her home. He must have made a good impression on her farming family, although someone with land would probably have been better.

My mother came from a long line of Tyrone farmers. They had been granted their land by King William when he was trying to take over Ireland. According to family tradition, the Booths came from Holland and were distantly connected with the Gore-Booths in Sligo — but that may have been just rumour as the Gore-Booths owned the neighbouring land. When Elizabeth saw my father she had just left a boarding school for young ladies in Cookstown — all the country girls went to it. She was celebrating her release by staying with another escapee in Magherafelt, before returning home to the depths of the country. In those days there was no question of looking for a job. Liz, like all young ladies, was destined to remain at home until a suitable husband appeared. She had not long to wait.

Joe's aim was to marry Liz quickly, but it would have taken a miracle to achieve that ambition. He could not afford to support her. He had just enough to meet his own requirements, as civil servants in those days were notoriously badly paid.

But fate took a hand. Joe found out that a desirable Post Office was becoming vacant in Bangor. But he knew nothing about the work and it was altogether different from the Public Works. I don't know how he wangled it, but he was appointed

— much to his astonishment. The principal attraction of the job was the house attached to the post. Such was my parents' delight that they didn't ask what the house was like.

All family objections were pushed aside — Liz being too young, the house to be furnished and Joe learning the rudiments of the job. It was a gift from the gods and the preparations for the wedding were put into motion. Liz was not the sort of girl who wanted to splash out on a big white wedding. "I'd rather have the money," she said. But I'm afraid that was wishful thinking. Maybe she'd forgotten her Papa was so close-fisted. In any event, he gave her only five pounds for her trousseau. Maybe that was a lot of money in those days, but I "hae me doots." My planter grandfather was notoriously mean and dedicated to buying back land that his forbearers had sold to pay for riotous living.

My mother was a wonderful story-teller. Times without number and as a special treat we persuaded her to describe their wedding feast. Invariably in my mind, I link it with the wedding feast of Cana. Or some great banquet in the time of Henry VIII.

"The preparations went on for weeks beforehand," Mumper would begin, delighted to tell the story yet again. "Everybody, just everybody, was to be invited. The whole countryside. . . ."

It became so alive in my mind, I felt I was there.

"The only suitable place for the event was the Big Barn," she continued. "That was a lovely old building, very large, high and airy, just the job, in fact, and in addition the wooden floor was suitable for dancing. Of course it had to be cleaned and scrubbed and polished. The men did that to your Grandmother's satisfaction, and she was hard to please, they said. Collapsible tables were borrowed or hired as were linen table cloths, white as the driven snow. And then the real work began, the baking and cooking — for it was to be a real feast and nothing like a wedding nowadays."

Time and again she told us, the actual wedding took place in Cookstown, where Joe had spent the night in a small private hotel. No doubt he had inspected the church beforehand. It cetainly didn't conform to his idea of a church. It was plain and unadorned, there was no musical instrument, no organ or even a piano and no pulpit, certainly there were no flowers — my mother's family were austere Presbyterians.

The ceremony was timed for eleven o'clock in the morning and only family was invited to that. Prompt to the minute, they all arrived and Joe and Liz were instructed to walk up together to where a man in a black gown awaited them. Liz was not permitted by her church to carry flowers and nobody gave her away, but she did wear a pretty blue gown and hat. The ceremony was completed in about twenty minutes, very plain and solemn. I don't think Liz ever got used to the Church of Ireland, as she rarely went to church. She said it confused her, which must have been a bit of a disappointment to our church-loving Dad.

After the service they went back to Joe's hotel for a light luncheon and the drabness of the marriage ceremony evaporated. They were joyfully man and wife and nothing could alter the fact. Moreover the real wedding celebrations were yet to come, without any puritanical presence to spoil the fun.

As my mother told us about the food they had prepared, I pictured a sumptuous feast. There were birds of course; chickens, geese, turkeys. There was roast beef, lamb, pork, varieties of vegetables and the inevitable potatoes. I don't think they had got round to salads in those days. There was soup and pudding galore, and of course, cakes — small and large — decorated with skill and a superb wedding cake. A truly wonderful feast, fit for the gods, enough to feed the biblical five thousand.

And the drinks were of necessity non-alcholic, or were purported to be.

"People brought their own bottles," Mumper said.

"Didn't your father mind?" I asked.

She laughed. "No, not as long as he hadn't to pay for them!"

This was another example of our grandfather's meanness.

The proceedings were scheduled for six in the evening and that gave plenty of time to congratulate the happy couple and to proffer wedding presents.

"Guests came literally in their hundreds." Mumper looked dreamy.

It was an exaggeration, I suspect. But they arrived in all manner of conveyances; from traps to gigs, to waggonettes until all available space was taken up, the stockyard and the approaches, even down to the meadows. I suppose all the animals had to be unharnessed and put somewhere.

"Such a gathering was never seen in mortal memory," she went on. "And all were dressed in their best grandeur."

She told us the guests exuded a smell of camphor from garments that had not seen the light of day for many a year. Rich and poor, the gentry and their servants, the ordinary farmer and his buxom wife, the townees from Cookstown or Coagh or Stewartstown or Magharafelt or even further afield. They were all there, Protestant and Catholic alike. Not to mention the fiddlers and other musicians.

And so at last, they were all safely gathered in. The rich and important and family friends were allocated to the tables near the front. Servants and lesser breeds, happy with their lot, were further back. They may have sat in different places but there was no difference in the food served to one and all.

Perhaps it was the custom of the day, but the family and relatives came in last. It was quite a ceremonial entrance. Lastly, came the bride and bridegroom to an accolade of cheers and noises and a rendering of "Here Comes the Bride", the fiddles drowned by the hearty singing and clapping and naughty remarks. It must have been wonderful.

"Who said grace?" I asked.

Mum couldn't remember whether anybody did. But she definitely said, "There were no clergy present."

I supposed that was on purpose because of the mixed multitudes, "All sorts and conditions of men," truly. There were speeches of course and poor Joe had to stammer out something. The father of the bride surprised everyone, his speech was funny and short, as all good speeches should be.

The feast lasted a long time but at last everyone was satiated and willing hands dismantled the tables and one could hear the far away sound of washing-up. The ladies disappeared to "make themselves comfortable" and the men disappeared somewhere else — there was plenty of room.

The sound of music soon recalled them all to the transformed barn. It was now a ballroom of a sort. There was an orchestra in full swing and soon the floor was full of merry dancing figures. Square dances were popular and I think even Queen Victoria would have approved although she was already an old lady by then.

But, alas all good things must come to an end and the coachmen and drivers were soon sorting out their horses and vehicles, but not before the traditional serenading of the bride and groom, accompanied by ribald remarks, to their bedroom. They had the good sense to lock and bar the door before they were actually put to bed. That embarrassment they were spared, forewarned by my grandmother.

One can but wonder what happened behind those doors. Of course my mother didn't tell us that. She was a virgin, I know, and I expect my father was likewise. So I suspect that they just fell into each others arms and laughed and laughed, tired and happy like two children. In a way it was all they were. Maybe they said their prayers, meekly kneeling by the bedside. I wouldn't be surprised. My father was by nature a religious man and was to remain so all his life, in a strictly orthodox manner.

My mother would entertain us till her voice wore out. And we never tired of hearing about the wedding. It was a great start, but life is, after all, what you make it. My father had just celebrated his twenty-fourth birthday and my mother must have been nineteen or twenty. I don't know whether they slept that night, but they were up and away early next morning ready to begin their life together. Not on a wasteful honeymoon, but in their very own house, scrubbing and polishing and painting, trying with some success to make an old house habitable. It must have been hilarious, for neither of them had the slightest idea of how to do such things. It was by guess and by God, my mother always said.

3

In time we moved from our first cockroach-ridden house to a new one over the post office on the main street of Bangor. Although about six, I can't remember the removal. But it must have been chaotic, as my mother wasn't the best organiser. I can see that tall house still in my mind's eye and walk through the rooms as if it were yesterday. The living quarters didn't start until we climbed the stairs which were just inside the front door. At the top of the stairs there was a square hall with doors which opened into the kitchen, the bathroom and the boxroom. A landing led to the front of the house and the morning room and dining room. On the next floor there were five bedrooms.

The kitchen was the warmest room because of the big black range and we always had our breakfast there. It was typical of the time. There was an old pine dresser, which held all manner of things and the cupboards underneath were full to overflowing. In the middle of the floor stood a scrubbed wooden kitchen table with six wooden kitchen chairs, some of which had arms. Two bookcases hung on the wall, full of cookery books and beneath them was a shabby leather sofa. The pantry had a cold stone floor and lots of shelves to store things. And the scullery was large and bare with only a mangle to decorate it.

The door from the scullery opened onto a porch, which was packed with my mother's geraniums and other flowers. This led to our favourite place, a cement roof garden. It was our outdoor playroom, and was decorated by degrees with large wooden boxes, flowerpots and containers with flowers and shrubs — anything that would grow. My mother would have a garden at all costs, even an improvised one. From it we could just see into the grounds of Bangor Castle where there were trees and grass.

The morning room was a dump and a sort of nursery. The dining room, which was in constant use from lunchtime onwards, was ordinary, with chairs, a table, a sofa, a sideboard and a bookcase. It was the room in which we lived, moved and had our being. It had only one window and was snug on winter nights. The drawing room had three and except for visitors was only used on Sundays. The precious things were there and we thought it lovely.

My parents' bedroom was in front of the house and the baby's cot was there. My sister Nan and I were in a horrid back room, sleeping together in a double bed until we had to be separated. The rows would start once we got into bed — children fight, I suppose, because each child is different. Finally I got a room of my own and the baby's cot was moved in with Nan. One spare room was very grand and one middling grand. The house wasn't suitable for pets, so we had none — except for the canary that lived in a cage in the kitchen.

I don't think my mother ever willingly threw anything away. The boxroom was full of trunks, suitcases and boxes of all sort and description. It was creepily dark and a constant joy to us growing girls, especially on wet days when we would dress up.

"Where did you get that?" Mumper would say, going into fits of laughter at the sight of one of us parading around the house. She was a funny woman, always ready with a witty answer.

"Do you remember that hat Joe?" she'd ask my father.

They always called each other Joe and Liz, never mother and father or anything silly like that. Sometimes it was Joseph and Elizabeth and at those times we crept silently away. Thunder and lightening were in the air and we never knew where the bolt might fall. But they were awfully young at heart and hardly ever fought. My mother was a pretty woman, built sturdily for endurance, with masses of untidy pale silvery hair. On the other hand, my father was elegant, tall and slim with navy blue eyes, jet black silky hair and a cavalry moustache. He might just have been a bit of a dog before he met his darling. I can still see my mother chasing him round the kitchen table. They had such great fun. Theirs was a love story and we three girls were incidental, I suppose. But lucky, all the same.

In the right mood, my mother whistled like a bird — little trills up and down. It was a joy to listen to. I never hear anybody whistling now, is it a forgotten art? She was a joyous creature, with a touch of contrariness underneath. She didn't make friends easily and applied the same rule to her daughters. We were told continually that we had enough company in our own family. "Play with your sisters," she said. I'm afraid, she didn't think there was anybody in a seaside town fit to associate with. "Land," she said, "is the thing, if you haven't land, you're just a nobody."

My mother was essentially shy, but felt above the common herd. This superiority was probably ridiculous, but was a characteristic of northern people, especially country land-owners. She was a country woman and not geared to the industrial revolution. I don't know why we called her Mumper. On state occasions, she was Mum or Mummy, but never Mother.

We didn't take the same liberties with my father. He was Dad or Daddy, or sometimes Father, but that was only to show our displeasure over something he had decreed. It didn't take him long to learn the signs. My sister, Nan, was fair and lovely and jolly well knew it. Helen, the baby, was sweet with soft brown curls and great goo-goo eyes. "Ma's own chilo," we teased her. I suppose I was Daddy's girl. He and I had long "intellectual" conversations in which I was encouraged to use my brains. This disgusted my sisters who thought I was nothing but a show off. This was offset by my father's injunction, spoken loud and clear, "Don't heed the small fry."

My father didn't favour me, but my sisters thought he did. On the whole we were a happy and gregarious family, encouraged to think and talk for ourselves.

My father enjoyed his work. He was king in his own castle with no one to challenge him. As time went on, more and more small post offices opened — usually in one half of a grocery shop — for which he was responsible, in places as far away as Groomsport and Clandeboye.

Postmen were a constant worry, sober and not so sober. There were also other staff to worry about — telegraph boys, assistants (mostly female) cleaners, and staff who tapped out all telegrams in morse code. It seems incredible in these days of high technology, but that's the way it was. Bicycles were used intensively and I remember hand carts for despatching and receiving mailbags from the train to and from Belfast. They always arrived at the last minute and were preceded by shouts, of "Make way for the Royal Mail." It was a phrase with which I was very familiar and sounded so important. There was a doctor who lived near us whose name was Pope and he varied the chant to, "Make way for Pope and the Royal Mail!" He was a very large man with a loud voice and a strong supporter of the Church of Ireland, which added to the fun.

We were not encouraged to talk to the postmen, a nod and a smile was thought sufficient. But we did know Creswell. He was the most senior postman and the butt of all the others' jokes. I'll never forget the day he knocked peremptorily on the back door, against all rules. I was the one who answered the summons.

"I want to see the Boss," he demanded.

I did not ask him in, but left him on the porch.

My father was reading the paper after lunch in the dining room and looked up crossly, staring over his specs. "What does he want?"

"He wouldn't say."

Dad finished reading before going to see.

But he came back in fits of laughter, the vein in his forehead was throbbing — it always did this when he was amused. "The silly old goat! He came up to report the others for hiding his glasses. He was in a terrible state, he can't see without them, and guess what?" My father rustled his paper and sat down. "His wretched glasses were on top of his head!"

4

Dust was always beneath my mother's notice, but she could cook divinely and was always reading up recipes from cookery books and glossy magazines sent by her sister in America. So our cuisine was above the usual everyday fare. We were used to good food. Saturday morning was her day for baking. She made everything herself: tarts, brown bread, soda bread, buns, cakes. She put on a big white apron and did everything herself— I helped, but my tarts were always grey and badly pawed.

In those days the tradespeople climbed the steps to the back door where orders were solicited and delivered in due course. The butcher, the baker, and the candlestick-maker all came with great respect to the lady of the house. She accepted such treatment as a matter of course. Our favourite weekly caller was a furtive-looking little man, always wearing a large overcoat much too big for him with lots of pockets. It was a poacher's coat, Dad said.

"Does she want any 'chickets' the day?" he'd croak.

His refrain never varied. "Chickets" was a term that covered all manner of things from chickens and ducks to pheasants and game. My mother was a good customer: partridges, grouse and wild duck featured frequently on our menu. She always said you couldn't get the same value in the shops.

"No, indeed," agreed Dad, "and you're compounding a felony!"

Whatever that meant, it didn't stop Mumper buying from him. We missed the little man when he stopped visiting. But Dad said he was probably in prison.

It was queer, but our father always got presents of fish. Fish had to be cooked at once then, as there was no such thing as putting it in the freezer or even on ice. One day she was confronted by two or three dozen herrings. What was she to do? Waste was sinful. Then a bright idea struck — kippers.

A new dustbin was ordered, but oak shingles were a more difficult proposition.

"Never mind," she said. "Oak shavings will do!"

So the bin was filled with the so-called oak shavings and the fish hung, one by one, on a piece of wire which was attached to the sides of the bin. The shavings had to be set on fire in order to produce gentle heat and smoke. This was all done under the watchful eyes of the entire family.

Mumper secured the lid and placed a flat iron on top. "It will take two or three hours!" she said confidently. "There's no point in standing here!"

Reluctantly we left the herrings to their fate.

The next thing was a ring at our front door.

A policeman stood outside. "There's a fire on your roof, Ma'am," he said matter-of-factly.

And indeed there was. The bin was on fire. Buckets of water were immediately dashed on it, but it was some time before the lid could be removed. Some burnt cinders were all that remained of the herrings. There was an awful smell of burnt fish.

"The recipe was wrong!" Mumper wailed.

"What do you expect, if you don't have the right ingredients!" Dad said tactlessly.

We melted away before she exploded. It was all great fun — and anyway we didn't like kippers.

Monday was always washday. Horror piled on horror, as my mother and the "girl" in the scullery rub-adub-dubbed all day long. The smell of soap suds was everywhere and the mangle squeaked and rumbled depressingly. The floor was awash and wet clothes were all around — even boiling on the range. For lunch we had Sunday's leftovers. It was hell. Mum was always exhausted, while Dad brooded at the top of the table.

Then things came to a head. One Monday, he thumped the table. "It's got to stop, Elizabeth!"

It was like God speaking.

"Well, you stop it!" my mother thundered back.

My father glared, then pushed back his chair and stamped out of the room, saying over hs shoulder. "By Jove! I will!"

We all quaked, but my mother roared with laughter.

"That's it, children," she said, sitting back in her chair. "No more wash days here!"

And there weren't. She knew her man.

My father rustled up a decent little woman — he always knew of them. She and her son came every Monday after that with a handcart and collected bags of washing and brought it all back on Fridays smooth and clean and beautifully ironed. It was no joke. In those days little girls wore white drawers, white petticoats and dresses. There were sheets, as well as pillow cases, table cloths and God knows what.

No doubt, my father thought it worth the money. It was probably some exasperated man like him who invented the washing machine.

There were no nursery schools then, so we were taught spasmodically by my mother at home. We knew all about the cat sitting on the mat. We could repeat the alphabet at an early age and we knew that two and two made four. I remember distinctly "de Vere Foster's Copy Book" with its difficult loops, and that kind hearts were more than coronets and a stitch in time saves nine. We were rarely left unattended. If Mumper had to go out, there was always a maid charged on peril of her life to keep an eye on us.

One winter's afternoon, I can't remember why, we were left on our own for a bit, while Mumper dashed out. She was a do-gooder by stealth, so it was probably an errand of mercy — home baked scones for some needy soul. She had left us all in the kitchen with strict instructions to stay there. I can see us now: Helen, playing on the floor with her toys; Nan engaged in some work of self-adornment, or her idea of it; and myself, as usual, with my nose in a book.

All was peaceful until Nan said, "I think the fire in the range has gone out."

She raked it vigorously. There was a faint glimmer, but it needed a little coaxing to come to life. But that was not my sister's idea. We knew our mother sometimes used a drop of paraffin oil in an emergency like this. So Nan dashed into the scullery, returned with the bottle and poured the lot into the range.

We hadn't long to wait for the explosion. I thought the house had blown up. But no — soot rained down on us. It was like black snow and we were turned into negroes. Everything was black: the walls, the ceiling, the furniture. And it kept coming. Helen was crying and the tears made white rivulets down her black face.

Our father was first on the scene. He dashed up from his office when he heard the explosion. He saw immediately what had happened and for once was speechless. Then Mumper arrived and, taking all in at a glance, began to laugh.

"It's not a laughing matter," Dad grumped.

But he had difficulty in keeping his own face straight. The soot was still descending and settling on them.

Oddly, nobody got into trouble. How it was cleared up was a mystery to me. We three were hurried into the bath — our hair was the worst. Meantime, Dad coped with the kitchen. As he said, it could have been worse. We could've been killed. But it was a long time before the kitchen was normal and the smell of soot remained until it was painted.

My father was convinced that nobody in Bangor could cut his hair properly. Or it may have been that he liked his solitary jaunts to Belfast, every three or four weeks. At any rate, it was quite taken for granted that his journey was necessary. On rare occasions, he took me with him. We looked forward to his outings because he always came home laden with goodies. There was a pork shop in Church Lane which sold County Tyrone pork. So invariably he bought ham or bacon and things like that — he wouldn't have dared to come home hamless. There was his special cheese, Roquefort, from S.D. Bell's and tea from Foster Greene's — it was *the* Belfast tea shop and very exclusive. We children had not yet developed a taste for the exotic, so usually there were sweets for us and other odds and ends. Our Dad was a man with no idea of money and spent anything he had.

The parcels were always dumped on the table unopened until it was convenient for Mumper to pass judgement and divide the spoils. On one occasion, we were poking and the cheese parcel came apart. It had a cheesy smell, but we didn't expect to see live cheesemites cavorting about. It might have been overripe, or maybe they liked it that way. But my sister Nan was horrified. I suppose, she thought we were going to be overrun with maggots, or that the cheese was bad. Her action was typically swift and to the point.

She scooped the parcel onto a shovel and threw it out the kitchen window onto the street below. Helen and I had no time to restrain her. We watched with horror as she hung out the window.

"Come and look," she called at last. "There's a boy down there with a teapot in his trousers!"

In our childhood there was no such thing as sexual instruction. There was no such thing as sex — you just arrived! And as there were no boys in the family, we knew nothing about the male body. We just looked at the boy. Then Helen, the baby, said, "I don't think that's tea. I think it's number one."

Nobody said a word about the cheese. And I don't remember how the teapot puzzle was solved. We didn't dare ask our Dad if he had one, but we definitely eyed him with a new awe from then on.

Throughout my childhood, we went for a daily walk in the interest of health. It was a family thing, we were never sent with a servant. My father was free in the afternoon, and came with us. Nan and I walked in front, followed by him and Mumper and Helen in a pram. I think they liked showing off their three girls. We always went to the country, never the sea to which Mumper had a rooted objection. They were extremely boring walks and one day, in a spirit of bravado, we purloined a halfpenny from the loose money on the kitchen sideboard and bought liquorice all-sorts from Mrs Murphy's sweet shop, two doors away. She gave us awfully good value, and so, fortified, we set off for our walk. The difficulty, of course, was to eat the delicious sweets without being seen and the amount of looking backwards to see if it was safe to pop another into our mouths was highly suspicious.

There was a reckoning — as soon as we arrived home, we were summoned into the kitchen. I remember Dad sitting on a chair and his back to the window. We were stood before him, one at each knee.

The dreaded questions were put. How? When? Why? Where?

We answered truthfully, of course.

"It's a sin," my father said gravely. "Even a halfpenny is stealing."

We mumbled in reply.

"God saw you," he went on. "Sin has to be punished."

I don't know where Mumper was — she was probably having a good laugh somewhere.

So God, in the guise of our Dad, produced a ruler from somewhere and we were told to hold out our hands. The ruler came down in a workman-like way on each little pink palm.

We yelled blue murder. But there was no comfort from anybody, so we fled to the privacy of a bedroom to compare wounds. That was the only time in my life I was physically punished. I've never forgotten the ignominy.

But events trigger memory and the shame of that punishment brings back the equal happiness of the next day. As if to wipe out our fall from grace, we were taken for the first picnic of the year. It was a lovely, spring day, sunny with a nip in the air. Everything was packed in a wicker hamper, a frying pan and a kettle went into a basket. Our destination was Helen's Bay and part of the treat was going by train. It was a short walk from there to a delightful, small glen with a clear stream flowing over shiny pebbles. The first primroses were peeping out here and there, also violets and buttercups. We gathered twigs and made a fire. Then boiled a kettle and fried sausages to eat with bread and butter. Did anything ever taste so delicous? Our shoes and stockings came off to paddle in the icy stream. Mum uprooted primroses for our roof garden. Then we put out the fire and, leaving everthing as tidy as we found it, went wearily back to the station.

The station master stopped the train for us — at least we thought he did. Then he blew his whistle, waved his flag and off we went. All the way home, trees flashed past. We arrived happy and dirty. I hope God was happy too and had forgiven us.

5

The climax of the year was our annual summer pilgrimage to Mumper's old home in County Tyrone. We lived for it, counting the days until the time came and always stayed for about six weeks or two months. "How long are we staying this year?" we'd quizz. "It all depends," we were told mysteriously — but to this day I don't know what it depended on. One particular year we went in July, a bit earlier than normal. As usual, we spent weeks preparing. Everything had to be perfect for the great day, so we wore our old clothes to save the clean ones. Even our dolls' clothes had to be washed, and the toys we were taking packed in a big wicker basket.

Then, oh joy, the black shiny trunk with the curved top was dragged out of the boxroom into the hall. It was big with leather straps and buckles galore. There was a removable tray inside which sat on top of the heavier things — it was for the dainty things, Mumper said. Then the clothes were gathered and neatly folded and piled in rows on the floor — some warm things, just in case, but mostly summer frocks. A great expedition had to be planned accordingly. It was not possible to travel light — endless trunks, holdalls and containers were necessary.

This all happened under the benevolent gaze of Mr Gladstone whose likeness adorned our hall. I'd only recently been told he wasn't my grandfather. Never having known one, I thought it a great pity. I'd looked at him every day for years. Now I wonder why he was there. My father wasn't political, but he must've been an admirer of that great English liberal whose mission had been to pacify Ireland.

At last the great day came. Under the anxious eyes of our

mother, the items of baggage were counted and recounted. Porters staggered and stumbled down the stairs and loaded them onto a horse-drawn van. We followed on foot, each carrying precious burdens. It wasn't far to the station. There Dad supervised the removal to the railway van of the train, while we waited anxiously in an empty carriage. Would he make it in time? But he always did. The whistle blew, the guard waved, and we were off. Carnalea, Helen's Bay, Craigavad, Cultra, Holywood, Sydenham — each station was anxiously awaited. Passengers got off and others got on, but nobody disturbed us and at last we puffed into the great big ugly Belfast station. Here the real fun began. We had to cross the city for the Tyrone train.

"You get a cab, love, and I'll see to the luggage," Dad said to Mumper.

And away he went, leaving her to cope with her three chicks. We made it to the row of horse-drawn cabs, each horse with its nose in a nosebag. Each looked more decrepit than the next.

"Cab, ma'am?" cried the drivers.

Mumper chose the least decrepit one — in those days there was no such thing as strict queuing like today. We were hustled into the musty interior, while she waited anxiously for the luggage. It arrived with a couple of porters and Dad in tow. Mum counted the pieces and, being satisfied nothing was missing, watched as it was stowed on top, at the back, or wherever it could be fitted. At last we were ready. Off we went, clippety-clop on the square sets of a very ugly street and then onto the main thoroughfare. We knew that at last we were in great, grey Belfast City, with its trams and shops and people.

At Victoria Street station it was the same thing — porters, luggage, tickets and an empty carriage for us. This was a big train, much bigger than the one we had left, with a big snorting engine. We watched as Dad saw to the luggage. This time Mum didn't even ask if he were sure there was nothing missing, when he joined us in plenty of time. Then, suddenly, with a great snort and rattle like a dragon awakening, we were off.

During the journey, we played happily or looked out at everything flying past. In due course, Mum produced sandwiches, and Dad told us stories. But it was a long trip. Helen fell asleep after whinging and crying and Nan and I were bored and cross and wanting to go to the W.C. So we staggered up the swaying train and, with a fit of the giggles, went together.

"When do we come to Trew & Moy?" I asked. The two names for one place had captured my imagination. It was a landmark which meant we were well on our way.

"How soon will it be to our station?" I asked again.

"Very soon," Dad said. "We've passed Cookstown. Next we'll pass Stewartstown. Then it'll be us."

He told us the train was to be stopped especially for us, so we felt important.

"Are we the only people to get out?"

"I think so," he said. "We must be ready when the train stops. We can't delay it."

All journeys end and so did ours. We were tired, dirty and hungry. Mum did her best to tidy us up for our Uncle Joseph who always met us. Then the train stopped with a jerk at our little station — out we all tumbled, and our precious luggage was thrown onto the platform.

With flying feet we rushed through the door to the road. Nan beat me to it, but I could see him. He was there, complete with horse and trap — Uncle Joseph with his twinkling blue eyes and crinkly fair hair just like Mumper, all six feet of him with arms outstretched, wide enough for two.

"How are my pets!" He swept us off our feet, brushed our faces with a straggly moustache. He smelt of tobacco with a hint of whiskey — the genuine "country smell," we thought. He wore his best Sunday suit and not the usual workday leggings with laces up the side.

We hugged and kissed him until he deposited us in the

shining trap. Then he kissed my mother and Helen and shook hands with Dad. They all piled into the trap. There was another conveyance — a gig, I think, for the luggage — and a lad, instructed to drive it carefully behind us.

After stowing the luggage, Uncle Joseph got into the trap and with a word to the horse and an elegant flick of the whip we moved off at a spanking pace. The thrill can't be described — it was sheer unadulterated magic. And my mother was in seventh heaven — this was her country and she was going home. Home. She began to whistle, making lovely music. The tune sounded familiar to me, but she said she made it up. Anyway, it was gay and fitted in with the empty road and the almost unendurable sweetness of the air. It was a beautiful summer evening. Luscious hedges, sweetbriar, meadowsweet, honeysuckle and hay gave off a perfume which could not be bottled and sold. The insects going about their business could be heard, and the occasional busy bee. The quietness was only disturbed by the clip-clop of another solitary horseman or a vehicle like our own and the cheery greeting, "Evening, Joe."

We passed a few whitewashed cottages. Women or children hurried to the door to wave and speed the traveller or satisfy their curiosity. Further on, we could see the occasional big house in its belt of trees with well-kept outhouses in the background — evidence of good husbandry. I envied in my childish heart the people who lived in such blessed fruitful surroundings.

At last we came to our turn in the road. It was somewhere between a lane and a drive and zig-zagged cosily to Uncle Joseph's house. But first we passed the huge iron gates of the overgrown drive on our right. Through the trees we could just see the ruin of a big manor house, the abandoned home of our mother's family.

It was an eyesore and reminder of past glories, so we averted our gaze and drove on in silence and there, round the next bend was the wide space and funny thatched house that we loved. It had once been the overseer's house and stood among trees, all sorts of trees, including plum. And at the door, waving both hands excitedly was Auntie Lily. She was small and slim and energetic. A child isn't aware if a person is beautiful or not, but she was probably very handsome. As always, her heavy red hair was on the verge of tumbling down over her shoulders, and her eyes were screwed up against the dying sun. "Ye're all welcome!"

We tumbled out. "Auntie Lily!"

In an excess of warmth and hospitality, we were hugged and kissed and pushed into the house.

It was the house that Jack built — an Irish cottage which had been added to, higgeldy-piggeldy, over the years. There was a long wide hall which meandered off to the right and left. The first door on the left was the kitchen door. Further on was a concealed shallow staircase and the dining room was just beyond that. Out of the dining room, there were a series of rooms, mostly bedrooms and Uncle Joe's office.

The other side of the house was the same — a concealed staircase and a room from which we were barred. Up each stairway were crooked corridors and rooms to which there was usually a step up or step down. It just went on and on.

"It's a danger to life and limb," Dad said.

Certainly no architect would have been responsible for it. Bits were built on haphazardly as they were required, probably by a handyman who at least knew how to keep the weather at bay. It was warm and dry with low ceilings and thatched throughout.

Nan and I were to sleep in one of the upstairs rooms. We were immediately dispatched there to get ready for dinner. It was all pink and white and pretty with a feather bed, and matching washhand basins, jugs, and chamberpots. A red-cheeked girl washed our dirty hands and faces and brushed our hair. Then, ready and starving, we ran downstairs.

Everybody was in the lamplit dining room before us. The big round table was set and delicious smells were coming from the kitchen. Uncle Joseph was carving a couple of plump chickens. Dad was carving a ham, and Auntie Lily was doling out roast potatoes, vegetables and gravy. Soon we were all tucking in as if we hadn't seen food for weeks. That was followed by pudding, gooseberry tart, I think. And so to bed, replete and almost asleep on our feet. I remember nothing more until the sun awakened me the next morning.

6

It always took a few days to get acclimatized to the farm.
First, we had to check that the piggery and the stables were
just as they were. Also the byre and barn, the huge stockyard
and haysheds, the hen houses and little river at the far end of
the stockyard. Then we had to go to the fields to see the new
calves. We had to see the cows being milked and big pails of
white foam being strained into shallow buckets so that the
cream would come to the top for churning. We had to find
out when churning was to be. We had to check if there were
any new men and boys. There were a thousand and one things
to see to, and the place was so big it took quite a time.

Nobody seemed in a hurry. Meals were never on time.
Auntie Lily wouldn't be rushed. She had her own idea about
time, and if she was baking, well, she could hardly stop in the
middle of it. Only one thing had to be on time: the men's
dinner. At twelve o'clock sharp they all shuffled through the
back door into the kitchen. It was huge with a flagged floor
and a large scrubbed table in the middle. There were guns on
the walls and an oak settle bed. There must have been a dozen
or more men to be fed. Mounds of potatoes were heaped on
platters in the middle of the table and the girls in the kitchen
attended to them and made the food for them. They always
seemed to have great fun, but we weren't allowed near. But
sometimes we were allowed go with the girls to take the men
their tea in the fields — strong, hot, sweet tea and freshly baked
griddle bread, dripping with butter and homemade strawberry
jam. The men sat under the hedges, eating and smelling of
sweat. And sometimes they let us have a bite.

Nothing edible was bought in Auntie Lily's house, except

salt and sugar — everything else was home produced. Sometimes we peeped into the store room to see the rows and rows of jam and preserved fruit, the sacks of flour and meal, the sides of bacon and ham strung from the ceiling, the sacks and sacks of potatoes, everything you could name. But the store was very, very, cold, not a place to linger in.

We weren't allowed into the dairy — unless we changed into clean pinnies and had scrubbed hands. Anyway, we only wanted to go there on churning days, which were twice weekly. The task required two men and a girl. The men took turns to hand churn the milk and the girl to make the butter. They skimmed all the thick cream off the top of the enormous shallow bowls that had accumulated for a few days. The left-over milk was given to the animals, then they churned the cream.

It was always miraculous to see milk turn into butter. Timing was the thing, they told us. The dairy man skimmed the butter off the top and washed and washed it under the cold running water, until all the cream was washed away and the pure delicious butter was left. To salt or not to salt, that was the question. It was a matter of taste. However, we had more interesting things to do and once or twice was enough. Anyway, little girls were only a nuisance in that stark place.

With so much to do, I was never alone. Sometimes one postpones a pleasure in case of disappointment; so it was some days before I could steal away to my favourite and secret place — my grandmother's wild garden. At last I stood outside the sturdy, heavy door in the wall that surrounded it. I pushed but it was stuck.

Luckily one of the men came along and heaved it open. "You don't want to go in there," he said. "There's nothing but a wilderness."

I looked at it in dismay. He was right. It was overgrown and that's why the door wouldn't open.

"Oh, but I do," I said.

"Well, leave the door open, or you won't be able to get

out." He scratched his head and, with a funny look, went about his business.

I stepped into paradise. Although overgrown, the garden was still lovely. It was very big and the surrounding wall was a delicate pink brick. The smell of box predominated. Originally, it had been laid out in a formal pattern, with lots of little box hedges enclosing square, oblong or round beds. Long straight paths led to the next part of the garden. Here were old fashioned flowers of every kind and a herb garden. Then came the kitchen garden — pears and plums grew on the walls, while enormous heads of rhubarb choked other things on the ground. And there were weeds, weeds, weeds.

Next came the orchard, apple trees, pear trees, crab apple, plums, damsons, gooseberry bushes, currants — black, red and white. And grass, waist high. There was a tiny pond where there used to be water lilies, and at the very end of the garden, bee hives. There was a little graveyard for beloved dogs. It too was now overgrown. What would my grandmother have thought? Although I never knew her, I felt the neglect would make her sad.

I was lost in a tall wilderness. But I could still see the white gravel paths. There were plenty of flowers, growing higgeldy-piggeldy, mostly big fat roses. And, oh, the intoxicating scent. It was lovely in spite of, maybe because of, its wildness. These flowers had all gone mad, proclaiming their beauty in tones loud and extravagant. Wanton, almost. When I got over the initial shock, I loved the garden's magic. I found a bit of green lawn and sat down to think, dream and inhale. It was an experience for an imaginative six year old.

I don't know how long I stayed there that day, but I didn't move until the sun went down and it was cold. Leaving, I put a stone in the door to keep it open. But small heads get big notions and, resolving to tidy it up, I went back to the house.

They had been looking for me.

"We're going to someone's house for supper," Auntie Lily said. "You have to have a clean frock."

41

She dolled me up and wrapped me in a shawl, because it would be cold coming back.

"Are we going to the tapioca lady's house?" I asked anxiously.

"No, it's the chocolate lady!" she assured me, laughing.

I remembered that tapioca pudding had been made for the children at somebody's house. But it was frogspawn and made me sick.

Everybody was waiting in the hall and the waggonette was at the door. Uncle Joseph wasn't driving. His head horseman sat on the box, whip and all at the ready. So we all bundled in with rugs and cushions. There were parcels that looked like bottles under the seats — nobody ever, ever, went to a party empty handed.

It was a long drive and we had to collect two more people on the way. As we got nearer our destination, we saw plenty of others going in the same direction. The house was large and at the end of a driveway and illuminated with soft lamplight. Many people could play the fiddle in my childhood and here somebody was playing a fiddle and a piano joined in. Maybe there'd be dancing and singing.

It was my first grown-up party. There were other children there, and to our disappointment, we were herded together in a separate room. It wasn't funny, especially when we could hear all the laughter and talking. So after a while one boy just opened the door and we all filed out behind him. There weren't many of us and nobody said a word. Nan and I sat in a corner like a couple of mice, hoping we'd be allowed stay.

Dad saw us and winked.

We listened to Auntie Lily reciting her party piece, 'Lord Allen's Daughter':

> "Come back, come back," he cried in grief,
> Across the stormy water
> "And I'll forgive your highland chief.
> My daughter, oh, my daughter."

She could recite reams and reams of poetry and should have been on the stage. Then Uncle Joseph stood up for his, 'The boy stood on the burning deck. . . .'

A few other people sang. Everyone did their party piece. Then the music started and Dad and Uncle Joseph came and whirled us round the room.

Afterwards, we went back to our corner and didn't dare move out of it all night. I remember someone took us to another room for chocolate cake and lots of lovely things to eat. Maybe we eventually went to sleep, because I don't remember much more. Except going home, with my Dad's arm around me. It was cold and there was a baby moon and even my Dad had the "Country Smell." Also, the ladies were pinker than usual and a good time was had by all.

The next day Auntie Lily found she was out of sugar.

"Somebody's stolen it," she stormed. "It's never happened before!"

So Nan and I were dispatched with Maggie, a sixteen year old maid, to Mrs Badger's shop. It was only a cottage, but the only shop for miles, and a long walk for little legs on a summer's day. But we wanted to go.

Mrs Badger sold everything — "hosiery, hams, collars and clams, laces and fans, dishes and pans." There were more sacks of things outside the door, as well as inside. She was a stout, red-faced, good natured, country woman who knew her onions — literally as well as figuratively.

She greeted us with smiles and a poke each of black balls — these were sweets wrapped in a cone of paper.

As we sucked the delicious sweets, she shook her head at us. "Are these wee girls to walk all the way back?"

Maggie nodded. "Aye."

"Go out back, Maggie, and call Paddy! He's up the field. He can take you back in the donkey and cart."

Maggie didn't need a second telling.

Paddy duly appeared, a strapping red-headed fellow with

an equally red face. He was what Uncle Joseph called a "muckle-jointy of a fellow." Maggie and he were obviously old friends and he wasn't loathe to stop whatever he was doing and harness the donkey. The cart was open-ended with a plank for the driver and his lady friend. The children sat at the back, legs dangling. We had never driven that way before and it was fun. He left us at the top of the drive, whispering something to Maggie.

She was evidently impressed. "Well, what do you know? The pig man's coming tomorrow and nobody told me."

It was news to us too. We'd never heard of a pig man.

"Who is he? What does he do?" we asked together.

Maggie looked at us with scorn. "What does he do? He kills pigs, that's what he does. Everybody knows that!"

"But why? Who'd want to kill a poor pig?"

She looked at us speechlessly, her face getting redder and redder. "Do yous eat bacon?"

We nodded.

"And where does bacon come from?"

We gaped in shock.

"It comes from pigs!"

We didn't believe her.

"I'll ask Daddy," I said, looking worriedly at Nan.

"Don't dare, or I'll murder ye!" Maggie looked dangerous now. "It's a secret — and you mustn't let on!"

But why not?

"Just don't, that's all!"

But why?

Maggie got fiercer and fiercer. She stamped her foot. "You mustn't tell! Promise now!"

"All right, we promise."

"Cross your hearts and hope to die!"

So we did. But the responsibility of the secret was more than we could bear. We were so quiet, I expect our elders thought we had a touch of the sun. That night we whispered for a long time in our big feather bed. No matter what, we were getting up in time to see the pig man. He always came early, Maggie said. But nobody liked him and the sooner he was away the better.

We awoke bright and early and struggled into our clothes, then crept out of the house and into the stockyard. That was where the dirty deed took place, Maggie had also said. Because of the water. It didn't make sense to us, so we'd just have to see. The men were already there, but no sign of Uncle Joseph. There was a tremendous squealing of pigs.

We crept closer.

The dreadful pig man did not disappoint us. He was big and enveloped in a sort of overall with a belt round the middle. Stuck in the belt were all sorts of knives, some bloody. His bare arms were bloody too.

We watched in dread.

Another squealing pig was carried out with its four legs in the air. Then two men held it, while another pulled its head back by the ears. With one quick stroke of the knife, he cut its throat and blood came gushing out.

We looked at each other. Was this what all Maggie's fussing was about? A pig being stabbed. I'm sorry to say, it didn't take a feather out of us. We just waited patiently for the next victim to arrive. Meantime the slaughtered pig was carried to an isolated building which was always kept locked. We wondered whether to follow it, or wait for more drama.

Then our mother came running into the stockyard, golden curls flying in the wind. "Has anybody seen the children?"

"Here we are, Mumper!" We ran toward her.

She looked relieved. "Oh, thank goodness! Well, breakfast's ready!"

Nobody asked us if we'd seen anything. It was a let down, when we were dying to tell about the poor pigs. And the horrible pig man. But it was considered an everyday event, rather boring.

There wasn't much more to do that day.

"Where's my sweetheart?" Uncle Joseph called. He never

walked anywhere and often whisked Nan away for a ride, which she adored. Now he threw her up on the saddle of his huge horse and jumped up behind her, cuddling her in his arms as they trotted smartly off.

I was afraid of horses and didn't envy her.

7

My grandmother's garden was my favourite place. I usually read there for hours and hours, blissfully alone. But one morning I decided to try and tidy things up. I started with the dog's graveyard.

I found a trowel in the dilapidated shed and began digging up weeds. But it was very hard work. There were five or six graves, each with a little grey tombstone inscribed with the name of a dog — Rover, Spot, Jock. I had done quite a few, when further on, something white showed through the long grass.

I pulled and tugged the grass away to find a white marble tombstone which said:

BROTHER ANTHONY
Requiescat in Pace

For ages I sat, looking at it. What did it mean? Was it a dog? But wasn't Anthony a person's name? And who's brother was he? Was he Uncle Joseph's and Mumper's? But, if so, why had we not heard of him. He might have been a child like me. Finally, I went to look for my Dad — he'd know.

He came back willingly with me.

"What a mess," he kept muttering. "Somebody should tidy the place up."

I showed him the tombstone.

He gazed at the words. "My goodness."

"What does it mean?"

"Well, Anthony's usually a man's name. But *Brother* Anthony? And no surname. That's a puzzle now." He rubbed his chin.

"Maybe he was a beggar," I said.

"No . . . " He shook his head. "He can't have been. A beggar wouldn't have been given such a handsome stone."

It was a beautiful stone. "But what does Req — req — ?"

"Requiescat in Pace? That's Latin and it means "Rest in Peace." Then Dad looked around at my wild and beautiful garden. "Whoever he is, Muriel, he's surely doing just that in this lovely place."

I was still curious. "But why's it in Latin, Daddy?"

He shrugged. "Maybe Auntie Lily knows. We must ask her about it sometime."

Then he wandered off, picking raspberries and totally forgetting about mysterious Brother Anthony and his tombstone.

But I kept wondering who he was. It was several days before I could ask Auntie Lily.

She was working in the kitchen and hesitated quite a while before answering, "Anthony, now who on earth told you about him?"

"No one, I found a tombstone."

"Of course, he's been dead a long time. And people forget. Maybe someday I'll tell you about him."

And she did.

"First of all," she began that very evening before bed, "remember that Uncle Joseph had seven brothers, all of them older than he. And four sisters. Your mother was the youngest of them all."

"That's a big family," I said, imagining the crowds of children who played where we played.

She nodded. "Twelve. And a wild bunch, I was told. All coming so close together. Well, one Christmas Eve, the coldest winter that anyone could remember, your grandmother and grandfather were sitting cosily by the fire, a great turf fire, in this very room."

I pictured my grandmother and once more felt close to

her because of her garden.

Auntie Lily's voice went on, "Outside, the snow lay deep and crisp and even, just like a Christmas card. They were probably having a late cup of tea. When suddenly, there was a faint tapping on the door. 'Who could that be?' asked your grandmother. Your grandfather, of course, thought it was her imagination. After all, it was snowing outside.

"But then it happened again. Not a loud knock, a soft, frightened, timid sort of knock. They looked at each other. This time there was no mistake. 'Open the door,' said your grandmother. 'No! Lord God Almighty, it's midnight!' said your grandfather. 'But it's Christmas. Besides it may be someone in distress!' your grandmother argued. 'We'd better see.'

"So they both went quietly down the hall and unbolted the door. They opened it an inch or so and peeped out. Outside was a body. It pressed against the door, and fell at their feet on the doorstep.

"'It's a tinker!' said your grandfather.

"'I don't think so,' said your grandmother. 'Look at his hands. Come on, let's get him inside.'

"And then they saw the donkey cart deep in the snow. Your grandfather was not pleased. He was very put out indeed. But between them, they carried the stranger into this very room and laid him on that sofa. He was light and slim, with long black hair, too long and his face was white as death.

"'Get the brandy,' ordered your grandmother. Then, with a teaspoon, she tried to force a few drops through those pale lips. Presently he opened his big brown eyes and mumbled, 'Pedro.'

"'What?' whispered your gran.

"'Pedro — my donkey,' he moaned, lapsing back into unconsciousness.

"'Hmm, I'd better see to it!' grumbled your grandfather. 'The brute's probably frozen to the spot.'

"After a while, he came back. 'Well, I've got it into the

stable and given it some hay and water. It'll be all right there.'

"Your grandmother was lookimg anxiously at her strange visitor. By this time she'd got some of his cold wet clothes off and wrapped him in blankets. A bit of colour had come into his face and he was coughing something awful.

"'Do you know,' your grandfather went on, puzzled. 'The cart's full of books. Old books, by the look of them. The fellow's certainly not a tinker.'

"The visitor coughed again.

"'Oh, dear,' she said. 'He's not much more than a boy. And a foreigner at that.'

"Then the grandfather clock in the hall struck twelve. It was Christmas Day and the man in the blankets tried to sit up and cross himself. Your grandparents looked at each other. 'Glory be to God,' said your grandfather. 'He's a papist! A foreign papist!'

"Your grandmother stood up. 'He came upon a midnight clear. We don't know *who* he is, or *what* he is. But he *is* our guest.'"

Auntie Lily lowered her voice. "When she spoke like that, your grandfather didn't argue."

"'I'll see if he'll swallow some hot milk,' your grandmother said, going out to the kitchen. And he did. It was well laced with brandy so he fell asleep immediately. They wrapped him up and, leaving him there, went to bed."

"Did he stay long?" I asked.

"I'll be coming to that," Auntie Lily said. "Well, as you can imagine, the children all got a great surprise when they came down for Christmas breakfast. They gaped at the young man on the sofa. He coughed a lot and said, "'Allo, 'allo.'

"'Did Santa bring him?'" your Uncle George asked.

"Your Gran looked thoughtful. 'In a way, I suppose, he did.'"

"But maybe Santa did!" I blurted.

Auntie Lily hesitated. "Maybe so. But it was a good answer, because she certainly didn't know where he came from. All she knew was that he was a gentleman. I don't know how she knew that, but she did."

"Christmas Day then wasn't like now," she went on. "Everybody only got one present. But Christmas dinner hasn't changed — it was still much the same. And people came from far and near to say Happy Christmas and have a drink. There must've been a lot of talk about our strange young man — they were calling him that already."

"Did they adopt him, sort of?" I asked.

She sighed. "In a way, yes. One more mouth didn't make any difference in that family. And anyway, he didn't seem to have anywhere else to go. And what's more he couldn't speak properly. Only a lot of old gibberish that nobody understood."

"A foreign language?" I asked.

She nodded. "Probably Italian, and as day succeeded day, he was always leaving, but your Gran always said, 'Wait till Spring.' I don't think she ever meant to let him go, because she loved him and he loved her. He called her his beautiful Signora, and kissed her hand. And she kissed the top of his head. He was like a bird on the wing, hovering, but never going."

"Where did he sleep?" I asked.

"They fixed him up with a room. I'll show it to you sometime. He withdrew into it and never bothered anybody. And all the time he was learning to speak English — at least the English we speak, which is a bit different. And he studied his books, which were now in a bookcase in his room. And a wooden cross hung on the wall. He was holy your gran said, and everyone wondered if he was going to be a priest when something happened to stop him."

"Did they ever find out?" I asked.

"No, he never told them."

"He followed your Gran everywhere," Auntie Lily went on, "and, I suppose, he learned far more about his new world than she ever guessed. How it came about, I don't know, but soon they set up between them a sort of schoolroom. The boys had got far too big for Master McGrath's little school — which was very primary indeed. So they only laughed at him. Your grandfather, who was very mean about money, said it was too expensive to send the boys to boarding school. It was different for the girls — they were sent as a matter of course to a Boarding School for Young Ladies in Cookstown. His hope for each of them was a good marriage. The boys were to be unpaid labourers, I suppose — but they thought differently.

"And as a sort of make-do in the meantime, a large room was transformed into a schoolroom and Anthony volunteered to do a temporary job on the boys. At least it would keep them out of mischief for a few hours. And the extraordinary thing is — it worked. Almost at once, he had them under control by the sheer weight of his personality. As it turned out, it was a two-way experience. They taught him and he taught them. Certainly, Mathematics, Greek and Latin were on the curriculum. As well as music and general knowledge. I don't think they'd have passed any examinations but they learned a lot and their respect for him increased.

"But there was a restlessness in the air. Everybody but their father knew that they couldn't be couped up forever. Something had to give. And in a way they weren't surprised when William disappeared."

"Who was he?" I asked.

"He was the eldest — your uncle," Auntie Lily went on. "I expect Anthony helped him. And in those days, there were great opportunities for young strong men in Canada and the United States — cheap land and hard work paid off. William went to Canada and in due course the next six followed. They peeled off, like the skins of an onion, one boy after the other. Your Uncle John has a tobacco farm in the Caribbean. He's done awfully well. He married a Donegal woman. Auntie Ruth."

"Granny must've been lonely," I said, imagining all the grandchildren she would never meet.

Auntie Lily looked sad. "She was. Because people went

away forever then. But, in the meantime, Anthony inspired her with the idea of a herb garden and real garden full of flowers. There was the orchard already, but that was not enough and it had to be improved.

"It was a clever move because it occupied her mind. She didn't have time to think of her sorrow. It was very unusual for a farmer's wife to have a beautiful garden, you know — usually on a farm there was no time for gardens. But Brother Anthony planned it meticulously, in the Italian manner. And he showed her how to make simple herbal remedies from plants and flowers."

The story of Brother Anthony was like a fairy tale. Auntie Lily told me more in little bits. I reminded her to show me his room. It was away in a corner of the house and still kept locked. She took a key from the door lintel and opened it. It was a medium sized room with a single bed against the wall and a wooden cross above it.

There was a small wardrobe and a table and two small arm chairs and two plain wooden ones. A washstand with a plain white jug and basin. A large bookcase was crammed full of books and a violin case was in the corner. There was a fireplace, of course, and heavy red velvet curtains. It was a nice room, with a faint scent of flowers and incense.

"Nobody ever went there, unless invited," Auntie Lily said. "He looked after it himself."

The schoolroom was next door. It was very plain with wooden chairs and tables and a blackboard. Also the inevitable bookcase, a capacious cupboard and very bedraggled-looking harmonium. Several maps hung on the walls. I imagined the pale young brother and my noisy boy uncles, all flown away now like swallows. If I listened hard maybe I could hear them now.

"Poor Brother Anthony faded away young," Auntie Lily said sadly.

"You mean he died?"

She nodded. "He didn't live to a ripe old age."

53

"What'd he die of?" I asked.

Auntie Lily shrugged. "Who knows? Maybe lack of Italian sunshine. Or maybe he missed his own people. He was always a bit of a mystery."

"Didn't they ever find out more? Why he came? Where he was going that cold Christmas night?"

Auntie Lily locked the door again. "Your Grandmother might've known. But she never told."

"But why not?"

"Maybe she promised not to." Auntie Lily's voice was low and she had a faraway look in her eye.

The story made my grandmother's garden even more magical. Now it was Brother Anthony's as well. After that I tended his grave and put flowers on it every day.

"Rest in Peace," I whispered into the earth over him.

It wasn't sad at all.

8

Because of these summers, in my childhood the word holiday was synonomous with happiness, and happiness with the country. It always seemed to be bright there. The sun always shone. Even the roads were white, not grey. I can't distinguish if something happened on one summer or another. The years sort of blur into each other. I know we went every year between July and September. My father commuted from Bangor for weekends. He absolutely adored my mother's people. I suppose he was a bit of a waif like Brother Anthony and they took him in.

One year there was a surprise.

"If you're good," Mumper said. "And if it's a nice day, we'll all go to 'the Field' on the 12th of July."

"What's 'the Field?'" I asked her, puzzled.

"It's a wonderful picnic," she said. "Run by the Orange Order."

I had heard vaguely of it, but didn't know what it was.

The Twelfth was sunny and we set out early. It took a waggonette to hold us all, along with all our hampers of food and goodies. It was to be a proper picnic with a proper tablecloth and everything. The journey was a long one and many, many fellow travellers were going the same way. Also many Orangemen, gay in their collarettes and sashes with banners and bands galore. In those days it was truly a national holiday for everyone, regardless of family background or creed. It wasn't political, as far as I knew. Both labourers and farmers, catholics and protestants seemed to be on good terms and all set for a good day.

I remember the heat especially — the weather was boiling.

The Orangemen in their Sunday suits and bowler hats looked distinctly uncomfortable, but the women were in cool frocks and straw hats. Everyone wore hats then. We had straw bonnets, while my Dad and Uncle Joseph sported boaters. These got pushed further and further to the back of their heads as the day wore on. There must have been hundreds of people there, all spread out on the grass, eating, drinking or sleeping.

We found a lovely shaded spot under a tree. Then the tablecloth was spread out, with all manner of goodies from the hampers. It was a real honest to goodness picnic — chickens, ducks, ham, homemade bread with butter and jam, cakes, lemonade, and fizzy ginger ale. In the distance, some men were making speeches and we could hear them shouting away. But no one paid any attention. Everyone was too busy enjoying the day. Children ran about. Girls and young men were laid out in couples under the hedges. We wondered what they were doing, lying there, cuddling each other.

"Don't stare at them!" Mumper said firmly. "Leave them be!"

"But what are they doing?" we asked.

"None of your business! Get on with your lunch!"

My father and Uncle Joseph bought beer from a cart, but we had homemade lemonade. It was delicious. I suppose we had to be taken behind trees after that, I don't remember. At any rate, everyone was in the same boat.

It was the only time in my long life, that I ever went to "the Field" and, although it was such a happy day, there was an undertow of tension. A sensitive little girl caught whiffs of it. It was like smoke from a dying fire which had been doused with water, seeping through the dried grass and drowning out the other smells of horse dung, honest sweat, cheap scent.

The speeches droned on and on, getting more and more passionate. Neither Uncle Joseph nor my father belonged to the Orange Order, I know. Maybe we'd come because they wanted to see what it was like. They sat in a huddle with half a dozen other well-dressed men. As the speakers shouted, they looked sad and weren't laughing like all the other people.

But the meeting ended without incident.

The bandsmen collected their instruments, the banners were unfurled. The Orangemen put on their bowler hats and moving into straggling line walked off the field to the beat of the Lambeg drums playing "The Ould Orange Sash."

Then they went into "Derry's Walls", ending with a solemn brass band playing of "Rock of Ages."

And that was "the Field" as I remember it all those years ago, a mostly happy carnival. People were out to enjoy themselves. Except for the hysterical speeches, religion and politics seemed to have no place in it. It was just a great national holiday in County Tyrone. How were we to know that the doused grass would one day kindle and burst into flames? What did the Lambegs' sinister rhythm say? Was it an ominous warning of things to come?

And so we went tiredly and happily home that day. Back to the big dark kitchen with its scrubbed table, wooden chairs, and oak settle, past the dairy into the privvies at the far end of the yard.

The kitchen was full of big men, talking with filled whiskey glasses. The Ladies retired to "the Room" and closed the door. It was the best room in the house with old beautiful polished mahogony furniture and the work of past generations displayed in tapestry and fine needlework. As the gentle clink of crystal came faintly through the door, the children, unwanted for once, went to see the piglets, slide down the hayricks, paddle in the little river, or sit quietly and sing and dream in Granny's wild garden. There were so many things to do until Mumper called us. A Mumper slightly flushed and giggly and like the other ladies, smelling of port.

It was always the same visiting relations in that beautiful prosperous county.

Soon after that our Uncle Joseph went to a sale. We didn't know quite what this was, but it was something to do with land.

"He has a passion for land," Dad explained, pointing to the wide well-tended fields. "You see the family once owned all the land around here. But they lost it so Uncle Joseph's buying it back bit by bit."

"How did they lose it?" I quizzed.

My father shrugged. "Oh, it just happened."

We also loved the countryside and wanted Uncle Joseph to get it back. But Auntie Lily was in a funny cross mood that day.

"Land, my neck!" she muttered, slamming from the room.

She was only interested in restoring the Big House. It was the wreck in the middle of the trees, with weeds growing inside it and birds nesting in its chimneys.

"Land!" she muttered again at lunch time.

All day she was cross, so we kept out of her way. But it was an established habit that everyone must turn up for the evening meal. This was usually between seven and eight in the evening — not an absolutely fixed time.

But, on that momentous day, Uncle Joseph did not come home. It was after eight when we sat down to eat and still no sign of him. There was "silence in the pig market." The look on Auntie Lily's face was awful. No one dared speak, except Helen.

"Where's Uncle Joseph?" she kept asking.

"He's at — ." But my father glanced nervously at Auntie Lily and his voice trailed away.

"I'll give you one potato, Helen," Mumper said, changing the subject as she spooned them out.

"I'm hungry!" my little sister wailed, insisting on two.

"Don't worry, Lily! He'll be home soon," my mother consoled.

Auntie Lily glared furiously from the sideboard where she was carving the meat. What was wrong with her? It was very disconcerting.

Mumper looked nervously at Dad.

At last we heard the sound of a horse trotting in the distance.

"There he is!" I yelled excitedly.

Auntie Lily's face was grim.

Was there to be a row? I was frightened and wanted to get under the table, but Dad laid a firm hand on my shoulder.

Then the door burst open and there stood my Uncle, all six feet of him, his face red and beaming. His hair was all askew and there was a strong "country smell."

"Well?" said my aunt sharply.

"Well, what?" said he. Then triumphantly, "Ballysallagh is ours again!"

"What?" She gaped in horror.

"Ballysallagh is ours again!"

In the flash of an eye, she threw the carving knife at him. Luckily he caught it, but there was blood on the tablecloth.

"You bitch!" he said.

And she flew from the room, shouting, "I won't live with you any more!"

We all shook in our seats. We'd never seen adults fighting before. Helen started whimpering. But my uncle calmly tied up his hand with his hankerchief, then helped himself to some of the pie we were having, ate it, and calmly excused himself.

We were hustled off to bed.

"A storm in a teacup," Dad said. "It'll blow over."

That night Nan and I snuggled together in the lovely feather bed between the lavender scented linen. As usual, we listened to the mice scampering in the rafters. And the wind sighing in the trees. Although we didn't actually say so, a longing for the sea breezes of home came over us. We'd been away a long time and missed Bangor and the sea.

The whole house was terribly quiet. Uncle Joseph always spent the evening after supper in his office at the back of the house. It was a small shabby room where he had his desk and books, black leather arm chairs, a couple of small tables. And his precious guns were on the walls. His dogs would lie stretched out on the hearth rug — actually it was the only room in the house they were allowed in. He paid his men there on Friday afternoons and on other days he talked to his men friends. We used to always hear loud laughter on our way to bed. Then loud discussions. There wasn't much in the county they didn't talk about.

Invariably our Dad was asked to join them and sometimes he did. But I think he equally enjoyed Auntie Lily's company. She recited poetry and sang songs in which we all joined in. She would've been a hit on the stage and was a wonderfully gifted mimic and story teller. Many a night she terrified us with stories about our banshee and the coach, driven, hell for leather, by a headless driver — an omen of disaster.

Had disaster struck now? There wasn't a sound to be heard in the whole house.

Suddenly Nan burst out laughing.

"What's so funny?" I asked.

"The look on Auntie Lily's face when he came in."

I laughed too. We talked and talked about what happened. And the more we talked the funnier it was.

Suddenly the door opened and Mumper came in, pretending to be cross. "Why aren't you asleep?"

"It was so funny!" I laughed uncontrollably.

Mum sat down and laughed too.

Then Dad appeared at the door, looking worried. "It was only a storm in a teacup. . . . "

But seeing us, he joined in the laughter.

The tension had vanished, so we finally fell asleep.

9

The next morning Uncle Joseph still had a neat little bandage on his hand. But otherwise breakfast was normal.

Even Auntie Lily was in great form. It was as if nothing at all had happened.

"It's such a lovely morning," she said cheerfully. "I think we'll go and see Grand Aunt Margaret."

This visit had been hanging over our heads for a long time. Grand Aunt Margaret was my grandmother's sister and lived in some style, they said, on the shores of Lough Neagh. I don't think she was very popular and it was a long drive. But it was coming near the end of our holiday, and maybe Auntie Lily wanted to get away for the day.

"Three children might be too much for her," Mumper said worriedly.

"Maybe we'll just take Muriel."

So it was decided that I would go with Mum and Auntie Lily — three visitors would be enough. There was no phone, so we couldn't let her know. But we wouldn't be taking her by surprise, as she expected us any day now. Life was like that in the country.

There was the scurry to get properly dressed and quickly away. Dresses had been kept in reserve for the occasion. I remember mine was pink. And I had a straw hat with a pink ribbon — everyone, of course, wore hats on state occasions. Mumper's dress was blue with a very long full skirt, while Auntie Lily's was green to match her green eyes.

The pony and trap were at the door and very smart they looked. Everybody was there to see us off in our grandeur.

"Be careful how you go, Lily," Uncle Joseph warned.

"That pony's very fresh."

She gave him a look of scorn. "Please don't tell me how to handle a pony, Joe!"

And she gave a flick of the reins and off we went at a smart canter. Very smart. I had to hold on tight. And I could hear the laughs of Uncle Joe and those we left behind.

But Auntie Lily soon had the pony under complete control.

Merrily we bowled along. It was a heavenly morning with blue skies and warm shunshine — just the day for a long drive. And it was long. I got bored and, having nothing else to think about, began to feel uncomfortable. The feeling got worse and worse, until I blurted, "I want to go, Mum."

"Nonsense!" came the reply. "Didn't you go before we started?"

I admitted to that and was silent for awhile until the situation became desperate. I'd wet my drawers. I knew it.

"Please, Mumper!" I begged.

So we stopped at the first gateway. To my surprise everyone decided to go.

We all got out and Auntie Lily tethered the pony to the gate with the reins. We each went separately to look for a bush to hide behind. I suppose it took a while, because when we returned to the gate together there was no sign of the pony and trap.

It had vanished.

We flew out to the road to see the trap disappearing into the distance, miles up the road.

"What are we going to do, Lily?" Mum asked.

But Auntie Lily had already started shouting, "Come back, here!"

We all joined in, to no avail.

"I'll try and catch her, Lily!" Mum said, hitching up her skirts and starting to run.

We all followed her. Mum and Auntie Lily ran with skirts held high. It was hot and we panted and sweated. Mum was in front as she was a very good runner, but her hat fell off and she had to stop to pick it up. Try as we might, we couldn't overtake that lively pony. What on earth were we to do?

Aunt Lily was nearly crying. "It's all my fault, I didn't secure the pony properly."

Mum gazed hopelessly at the horizon.

"I thought I did!" Auntie Lily broke into sobbing.

"Crying won't do any good!" Mum snapped.

Auntie Lily didn't stop.

Mumper became exasperated. "Oh, stop it! Stop it at once!"

I thought they were going to have a row.

It was awful.

"Oh, God, Oh, God," I prayed to myself.

And this is where the miracle happened.

Out of the hedge ran a barefooted boy, dressed in green of all things. He caught that pony and spoke softly to him and calmed him down, while we puffed up, completely breathless.

"Nice pony you've got there, Ma'am," he said as if it were the most ordinary thing in the world to catch a pony at full gallop on a lonely dusty road.

"Thank you very much," Auntie Lily panted.

But it was at me he looked, winking.

Why did he do that? Funny boy. Or was he a pixie?

Auntie Lily pressed something into his hand which he didn't refuse. "Can we give you a lift somewhere?"

"No thanks, Ma'm, I live just over the hedge." And he indicated the direction with his head.

But I didn't see a house there.

He was a funny boy. He gave the ladies a grave little bow and winked again at me. Mum and Auntie Lily said he was a gypsy. But I thought he was a pixie — sent by God.

Anyway, there was no nonsense from then on. Aunt Lily took the reins with determination. It was "Drive, James! And don't spare the horses!" And the pony didn't disappoint us. Maybe he smelled water and knew we were getting near the

Lough. We galloped on, passing groups of whitewashed cottages, very poor and untidy-looking. Outside the children were in rags and none too clean. I waved but they didn't smile or wave back, but just stood there, staring with fingers in their mouths.

I hadn't ever seen children like that before and asked, "Are they poor?"

"I suppose so," Mum said, and that was all.

But I wondered why they didn't wave.

We soon came to open iron gates and went up a long dark drive. Trees and laurels blocked all the sunshine and light. It felt creepy and we drove silently along. Eventually it opened onto sunshine and a large white house. We pulled up and a man appeared from nowhere. As we stepped down, he held the pony's reins, then led it away.

The front door opened simultaneously. A maid in a long black dress and snowy apron greeted us pleasantly. "Good day to you," she said. "The mistress is waiting."

I saw her disparaging glance at our tousled and wrinkled selves.

"It's a very long drive," Mum said, noticing it too. "We could do with tidying up."

It was the understatement of the year.

But the haughty maid took no notice and ushered us into the Presence.

My Grand Aunt was exactly like pictures of Queen Victoria. She sat in the same regal splendour, waiting to receive her subjects, her little feet on a footstool. She was a widow too, at least she must've been, because there was no man about.

As we walked over, she extended a languid hand in greeting.

I wondered if we were supposed to kiss it.

Then she laughed, breaking the spell. It was a really hearty laugh and we all joined in.

"What a set of scarecrows you look!" she said. "Go away and get yourselves tidied up!" She rang a little silver bell.

"We had a mishap," Mum muttered.

Auntie Lily added, "Yes, the pony —"

"You can tell me about it when you come back!" Grand Aunt Margaret waved them away.

I liked her from that moment. The self-same maid led the way upstairs to a sumptuous chamber — I couldn't call it anything else. It was all gold and brocade with a four poster bed and mirrors galore. There were wash-hand basins. And jugs of hot water and lavender soap and embroidered linen towels and even a commode. Everything was placed, ready for use by the ladies. And the ladies took advantage of this, giggling all the time.

Then we trooped back downstairs, now fit for inspection.

"Ah, that's better," conceded the lady from her throne.

Again I confused her with our late lamented majesty, although the Queen had been dead quite a time.

She graciously took my hand. "And which one is this?"

My mother introduced me and I stood there awkwardly, as the old woman inspected me.

Finally she squeezed my hand. "Not like our side of the house, I'm afraid. But she can't help that!"

I felt I'd passed the test, but only just.

"Now girls," she said brightly. "What about a little glass of sherry?"

And lo and behold, there was the maid again, at the ready with a decanter of sherry and four glasses on a silver tray. The old lady had a second glass, but Mum and Auntie Lily resisted temptation and contented themselves with one. I was allowed a tiny sip out of my own glass, but didn't fancy it much.

Then we silently proceeded to the dining room. Again I'd never seen anything quite like it. Everything was lovely. The table was laid with sparkling cut glass, shining silver, and napery and roses. Herself presided at the top, looking even more like the late Queen. I was too overawed to eat. I suppose I was afraid of doing something wrong.

"The child has no appetite," Grand Aunt Margaret told

my mother. "I hope she's not sickening for something."

My mother told me to eat up.

But I couldn't. So I really can't describe the menu now — except the pudding, which was apple tart. I was glad when the meal was over and I was allowed out to the garden, while the grown-ups had coffee or tea or something.

The garden was not very big and not very interesting. So I opened a gate and found myself on the shore of Lough Neagh. There was no sand, just grey stones and gravel. But there were some boats and fishermen. And the same sort of raggedy children we had seen before were playing there.

I waved, hoping they'd let me join them.

But they didn't speak to me, just stared.

So I wandered about, feeling out of place and unwanted. Finally I went back to the dull garden, wishing it were time to go home.

My mother and Aunt Lily must have had similar thoughts, because it wasn't long until they called me.

"Get your hat and say goodbye!" Mum said.

"Yes, it's a long way back. The evenings are drawing in," Auntie Lily was saying, "How quickly the summer goes."

How quickly indeed, my mother was agreeing with her. So the pony and trap were brought around. And we all kissed the old lady goodbye. She smelled of camphor and her lace cap wasn't quite straight.

"Come again, children," she said. "Come soon."

"We will," Auntie Lily and Mum said together.

"You know you're always welcome."

And off we went at a decorous pace.

Nobody said a single solitary word until we were well on our way. Then the two women giggled and laughed and words kept bursting out. I didn't know what they were talking about.

Then Mum said, "I suppose you're starving?"

I nodded.

"But why didn't you eat your nice lunch?"

Before I could answer, she produced a couple of squashed-looking buns. "I stole these for you. I hope she didn't see me."

And so we went homewards on that lovely summer evening. The lamps were being lit in all the cottages we passed, but there was no sign of the gypsy boy — my pixie. Although we looked for him. But thank goodness we didn't need him now. At home we got a warm welcome. You'd think we'd been away a week.

That visit was the grand finale of the summer. A few more days and it would all be over for another year.

"The best of the summer's gone," Dad said sadly.

It was true there was a nip in the air. Very soon we were on our way with even more luggage than we came with. Hampers of this and that, home cured bacon and ham, butter, eggs, even a sack of potatoes. I remember Dad looking more and more dismayed as the parcels increased.

That summer was our last trip to the country. Uncle Joe was killed soon afterwards. Dear, kind Uncle Joe. The story went that he was training a young horse which threw him, breaking his neck. But a political murder was hinted at. After all, Uncle Joseph was an expert horseman and had broken in dozens and dozens of horses. I said this to Dad.

He nodded. "It still happens. It can happen to anybody."

But I remembered those ominous Lambegs. Were they giving us a warning? It was a sad day for us. Our father went to the funeral of course and came back none the wiser. One of Auntie Lily's brothers seemed to be in full control. She was in no state to talk to anyone. But she was the sole legatee. The murmurs of foul play were quickly squashed. As far as we were concerned, it was the end of the matter. And it was the end of something for us. Later we heard a rumour, that Auntie Lily, as a wealthy widow, was being courted from left right and centre. She did eventually marry again, as was right and proper. None of us ever went back there again. Indeed we were never invited.

10

The journey back from that last country holiday has faded from my memory, perhaps because a cloud hung on the horizon — school. The topic had been discussed so often. Where would my parents send their precious children?

But there was to be a respite: I caught the dreaded scarlet fever. Although it was regarded as a very serious illness, I was nursed at home — people then didn't like to send their little girls to hospital. Fortunately I don't remember much about it. Nan and Helen were sent away somewhere and I was completely isolated. Sheets steeped in carbolic were nailed up outside my door and nobody was allowed in unless they were all covered up in overalls. I must have had a high temperature, because I kept seeing the oddest things. Mostly birds, with enormous heads and eyes, which frightened me.

But that fever passed like all things. One day I was carried downstairs and dumped in a warm bath and all the loose skin that was peeling off had to be removed — it was infectious they said. I had grown in the six weeks and I had long, skinny legs that wouldn't work properly. My mother and I were packed off to Newcastle, so I could convalesce. I remember very little about it, except that my mother hated it.

"The mountains are too near," she said. "They smother me. I feel they'll fall on me."

I wondered how she could think this. Looking back, she was probably bored with me. After all, she'd had a bellyful of nursing me. I don't remember much about Newcastle, except I was bored too and we didn't stay for the allotted time. So it was home again, jiggety-jig in the train. And there was never a more welcome sight.

Christmas came next with all its excitement. It was a time my father did not like. Apart from the extra work and the confusion, there was always the hazard of postmen who yielded to accepting hospitality of the liquid variety. He sympathized with them, of course, but duty and strong liquor was forbidden during working hours. At least that was his invariable sermon when a man was unfit for duty. Many a one was sent up to Mumper to be doctored with hot strong coffee. This almost always made the poor man sick and in short time he was declared fit. But if he were thought beyond treatment, he was sent home — which always meant extra work for the others.

Nobody was normal until Christmas was over.

Most of all my father hated personal presents with which he was inundated. Long and anxious thought was given to their disposal. Nothing on earth would have persuaded him to keep them. Finally he and Mumper wrote a polite note, saying, "The Postmaster thanks the giver very much but, as it is against all rules for him to accept presents, he has forwarded it to the Cottage Hospital" — or whatever charity it was deemed suitable for. My mother wrote all the cards and they were delivered by the appropriate postmen with the mail.

But those days leading up to Christmas were magic for us children — the cakes and puddings which we all had to stir for luck, and above all, the letters to Santa. We always took great care with writing them. Usually we did it in the evening when the dishes were cleared from the kitchen table.

"Santa hasn't as much as usual this year," Dad warned from behind his paper. "He has lots of boys and girls to think about, so don't be greedy."

But we hoped for the best.

The build-up was unbearable. Then not being able to sleep on Chrismas Eve itself. Hearing faint noises in the landing. Being scared to death in an exciting way. Then at three or four o'clock in the morning, fistling about in the dark and guessing what the things were. Our stockings were always tied to the bottom of the bed and there was always an apple and an orange in the toe of each, so that was no surprise. But, if we were lucky, there was a pillow case of toys for each of us. And the joy of getting what we wanted!

Christmas breakfast was very special. We always had it in the warm kitchen. I remember Mum and Dad laughing and having fun. Then bells pealing as we got ready for Church. Dad and Nan and I went, Mum and Helen didn't. Dad was always something special in church, so we had to be there early. And we left last along with the rector and curates.

Then home again to a big log fire in the drawingroom. We weren't allowed into the diningroom till later. Then we got more presents from aunts and uncles before lunch. Mum and Dad would have a sherry, which was very unusual. Dinner was at a funny time — usually three or four o'clock. It was dark with candles on the table and gaslight and lamplight everywhere.

The magic has remained with me all down the years. The scrumptious food, with all the right *et ceteras*. The pud and mince pies. The coffee and my Dad's luscious Havana cigars — a present from someone, I suppose. But above all, I remember the fun and love.

Someone must have cleared up — there was always help in the house. Then it was time for games — Charades and Hunt the Thimble. We also played a thing called The Wee Filory Man. In this we had to follow whatever the Filory Man did. If we made a mistake, or were not quick enough, we paid a forfeit. There was always quite a party. I don't remember who came, but everybody had to take part until we were sent to bed.

We wanted it to last forever. But over meant over. It was bedtime and business as usual until Helen's and my joint birthday on New Year's Eve. Nan cried most of the time because she was left out of this celebration. This is probably why I didn't like my birthday. It was a sad day and the very end of the year. Everything was dead or dying and the New

Year had not come. Even in church the hymns were sad:

> A few more years shall roll.
> A few more seasons come
> And we shall be those that rest
> In peace beyond the tomb.

Even the church bells tolled portentously.

I I

After the New Year, school loomed terrifyingly. We were to go to a local church school — for a time at least. It was called the Ward School, because it was endowed by a family of that name. I know there were fees, but they weren't deadly. I was seven and Nan was almost six, and we were considered very old to be going to school for the first time. But we could both read and write up to a point, so we didn't suffer the humiliation of having to start at the very beginning with much younger pupils.

Still, it was a sad little trio that set out that Monday morning. Mumper wasn't very good at hiding her feelings. I suppose she felt this was the first step in a final letting go.

We slowed down as we approached. The school building was two storey and quite large and square. We knew its appearance well from our daily walks, but hadn't cottoned on to the idea that it was to be such a part of our daily lives.

"Hurry, children," Mumper said with false cheerfulness.

Then, willy nilly, we were somehow inside the dreaded portals. It was quite nice really. There was a square hall and a shallow wide staircase with a nice curve in the middle, leading upstairs.

Miss Brice was waiting for us. She wore a long dark skirt and a white blouse and she had a notebook in her hand. She shook hands reassuringly with my mother. "Good morning, Mrs Breen."

My mother greeted her, looking absolutely miserable.

Miss Brice did not ask us to come any further, but started to note down the "particulars" about Nan and me.

"What age are you?" she asked.

We told her.

"Seven and six, imagine," she jotted. "Hmm. Quite old in fact."

I looked at Nan. Were we really old?

"And where were you born?" And finally, "What church do you belong to?"

She knew that perfectly well, but we told her again and that too went down in the little book.

"Well, now, I think that's all," she said firmly. "I'll just take the children upstairs and give them a few tests."

Mumper was being given her congé. She looked at us as if her world was ending.

Miss Brice noticed. "Don't worry, Mrs Breen. "We'll be good to them."

We watched Mum tail away home by herself, then walked up the wide stairs, hand in hand for mutual support. At the top there was a landing with a swing door facing us through which we were ushered to be met with a subdued murmur, like angry bees in a hive. To our right as we entered there was a very heavy green curtain which divided the whole of that floor in two. And the noise, we discovered, was the mixture of numerous children's voices, reciting their own particular lessons.

It was very disconcerting.

But Miss Brice ushered us through one end of the curtain.

"This is the Infants' side," she explained.

There was a sort of gallery to our extreme left and a raised platform in front of us. The middle part was composed of groups of children seated at desks. The place was a hive of busyness.

"Miss Anderson, could you spare a minute," Miss Brice called.

A long thin lady immediately answered the summons.

"These are the children we were talking about," she said. "I don't know where they'll fit in. You'll have to give them a few little tests." She smiled at us encouragingly. "I'm sure you know quite a lot."

We looked nervously at each other.

Miss Anderson took us to a little classroom and sat us down at desks with pencils and some paper and told us to write down, "This is a nice day." And some other things. Then we did some sums. Next she gave us a little book to read aloud to her.

"Now," she said, "that wasn't too bad, was it?"

We shook our heads gravely.

"Well, now. Let me see — I think you'll be happy with Miss Ellis, Muriel. And Anne, you'll be with me — until we see how we get on."

"Will we both be in Infants then," I asked timidly.

"Yes, for the time being."

Anne was delighted. But I, who had thought myself such a big girl, was only an infant after all. Anyway we were separated, one with each teacher. Miss Ellis was young with sandy curly hair and smelled of onions. But she smiled a lot, for which much can be forgiven.

That first morning was confused and neither of us liked it much. At lunch time we were sent home in the care of a big girl, as it was our first day. Real school, we were told, would start the next day and we'd better be there before nine o'clock. Assembly was at nine sharp and Mr McDonagh, the headmaster, wouldn't tolerate latecomers. We were to bring sandwiches for our lunch.

Back home poor Mum and Dad had to hear every single word about our day.

"It'll be better tomorrow," Dad said encouragingly. "The first day's always the worst."

I hoped that was true. But he was always right.

Morning came all too soon and off we went by ourselves.

"Be careful of the crossing at Warden's shop," Mum warned, nervously waving us off.

Warden's was a paper shop at the corner. It was one of

those old fashioned shops with two large crammed windows — the whole shop was cluttered with papers and things. "Jeemes," as everybody called the owner, never got rid of a single paper, except what he sold. It was almost impossible to get inside, as there was only a single gangway. Yet he had everything necessary in the way of stationary and always knew where things were. It wouldn't be allowed nowadays, as it was a fire hazard. "Jeemes" himself was tall and thin and beaky and his clothes hung on him. His tweed hat came down to his nose, which always had a drop at the end.

That day we crossed without looking in the window. Then, as we'd been told the School's front door was for the privileged, we went in the back gate to the tarmacadamed playground. It was cut off from the street by the railing, but anybody could look over it and see their children at play. Then we trudged up the cement steps, past the open lavatories. There were no doors on them, except for the last one which was locked — it was for teachers only. And so into the Infants.

"You sit here, Muriel. And Anne, you're in Miss Brice's class."

Memory is a picture, you don't just remember what people said. You actually see them. To this day I can see all those people from my school. At eight fifty-five a.m., precisely, the big green curtain was always pulled sideways for assembly. Then all the boys from downstairs came clattering up, followed by two or three masters, and sat down in the gallery.

We looked at them, but were unimpressed. Lastly came Mr MacDonagh. He was stocky and grey with a very red face, twinkling blue eyes and an air of authority.

We all stood up.

"Good morning, children," he said.

"Good morning, sir," we chanted back.

"This morning we'll sing the first verse of 'Onward Christian Soldiers'. You all know the words."

Miss Anderson was already at the piano. She was a long, lean stick of a woman, with long skirts — we later learned with glee that her name was, appropriately, Lena. So with full-belted enthusiasm, the christian soldiers marched figuratively to war:

> Onward, Christian Soldiers
> Marching as to war
> With the cross of Jesus
> Going on before.

That was followed by a full-throated treatment of the Lord's Prayer.

"Our Father, which art in heaven . . ." chanted so many children's voices.

And that was it. Assembly was over. The boys were then marshalled by the masters and all retreated noisily back downstairs. Mr MacDonagh bid a courteous good morning to the lady teachers and went downstairs the way he had come. By the front — no back stairs for him!

Mr and Mrs MacDonagh were the principals of the school and came from Mayo — much to the disgust of the local people, we were told. They had been brought there by Lord Clanmorris who, looking back, must've been a governor of the school. He came from Mayo as did his title. He was a huntin', shootin' and fishin' man, but penniless. So he married a County Down lady with plenty of money and lived in Bangor Castle. Maybe the school went with the castle, I don't know. But everyone liked him.

The MacDonaghs were another matter. They thought they were a cut above the local "peasantry." Whether they had any qualifications or not, I don't know. At any rate, I suppose they lent a certain cachet to the school because of their airs and graces.

Mrs MacDonagh didn't arrive until late morning, but everyone was scared stiff of her. She sat in style at a large table at the top of the big girls' section. Her hair was piled on top of her head, like Queen Alexandra, and she always wore navy blue with a high white lace band round her neck in the fashion of the day. She inspected everybody's hands and nails at least once a week and taught sewing very unsympathetically. She made it laborious and uninteresting. We started off with a square piece of white linen, called a specimen or sampler in the olden days, and on this we learnt the various stitches — running, hemming, backstitching. Each row was in a different colour, but mine was greyish black before long. After that came dressmaking, during which we were shown how to make garments. I made a chemise which would have fitted Finn McCool. It was never finished.

On the whole, Mrs MacDongah leant an air of elegance to the scene. Maybe she did more. I don't know. I only know she was very good at inspecting everything.

In the Infants' School, we were taught everything by rote.

"Seven times one are seven, seven times two are fourteen," we repeated over and over and over again. And so on, ad nauseam.

Writing was done à la Fosters' Copy Books — all proverbs: "A stitch in time saves nine" was in copperlate. The next line was a finely dotted tracery, which you over-wrote. And the next five or six lines you were on your own. There were pages and pages of different proverbs: "Too many cooks spoil the broth," etc. I can still see those children, sitting at the little desks, tongues anxiously licking lips as they did their best to copy the text.

Reading was easy but uninteresting. And arithmetic was dreadful. Long division I still remember with horror. As for Algebra and Euclid, they meant nothing to me, but these were later tortures.

Lunchtime was short and sweet. It was followed by games in the playground, which I loathed and detested. As there was no games' mistress, they were organised by Miss Ellis. I learnt later that she was an excellent tennis player — Captain of the team and all that.

I was becoming restive in Infants, so, just in time, was

promoted to the other side of the Green Curtain. This was called First Standard and I began to enjoy it to a certain extent. We learnt geography, which I disliked, and history, which I loved. I also enjoyed literature and my first attempts at writing an essay. But drawing reduced me to tears, they just dropped down my face. I wanted to do it, but couldn't. You were disgraced if you couldn't, so a kind girl called Savage always did it for me, rather than see me cry. I've always felt grateful to her.

We were taught Scripture by one of the masters and had to clatter down to the boys' school for that. I nearly always felt sick there. There was a funny smell which one of the other girls told me was the master's feet — such a pity, as he was a very good-looking young man.

Science too was downstairs. The joys of the bunsen burner, litmus paper, and all the other magical things were imparted by the head himself. The so-called laboratory was a raised platform behind Mr MacDonagh's desk. Everything was very elementary, I'm afraid, but exciting. Anything could blow up any minute, and indeed, that's what happened occasionally. The master too could blow up. Woe betide anybody who stood in the path of the tornado. I added a few words to my vocabulary, which sounded great, but did not appeal to my Mum and Dad.

Music was something to look forward to. "Doh, rae, me, fa, soh," could actually be written down. And to my surprise and embarassment, it was discovered I had a voice and a good ear. I was held up as an example to the class and this made me big-headed.

But my own family soon took me down again.

"A gift from God," Mum said, "and nothing to do with you!"

But I was good at something now.

Years later I came across a poem about the school, "Bangor, Spring 1916" by my dear friend, John Hewitt, who attended it some years later.

> In Bangor for some months I went to school;
> I now have scanty memories of the place,
> could point it out, but not describe one face.
> One instant only was it colourful;
> when Lord Clanmorris called, his face was pink
> as was his shirt, his tie; his hair quite white.
> The masters smirked and bowed and seemed to slink,
> standing in silence we enjoyed the sight.
>
> Headmaster, back from ruined holiday,
> told once of Dublin and its Easter Week,
> of the dead horses and abandoned cars.
> But of the politics of that affray,
> the seedbed and the source of future wars,
> he certainly made no attempt to speak.

I never heard Mr MacDonagh speak of politics either, but
1916 and its consequences were all in the future.

12

One morning I heard my parents arguing. At those times curiosity guided my feet to the scene of the action. When Dad was giving forth, it was always worth listening to and I guessed that he'd be addressing a one-woman audience — my mother.

Yes, she was receiving the full benefit of his peroration. standing with arms akimbo and fair curly head to one side. I was in time to hear her say. "But Joe, you didn't lift your hat!"

"I did not! I'll doff my hat to no man," my father proclaimed in accents loud and clear.

It looked to me as if she'd been egging him on for her own amusement. She was good at that.

"But he lifted his hat to you, Joe. And you just nodded to him. That wasn't polite!"

"Woman," he said. "I'll lift my hat to the lowliest woman in the town but a nod is good enough for another fellow."

It was true. I had seen my father on various occasions sweeping off his hat with a flourish Sir Walter Raleigh would have envied to our washer woman.

Those were the days when men wore hats and my father had a fine selection that decorated the stand in our hall. Caps for rough weather, a couple of weatherbeaten Paddy hats, a bowler for Sundays, a straw boater and a silk hat for weddings and funerals which rested in its own little leather case. The postmen, the telegraph boys, cleaners and other odds and ends tipped their hats to the Boss as a matter of course and received a nod in return. That was as it should be, but apparently my mother thought the same action was rude or bad mannered when Dad did it to others.

My father was one of these very good people with enormous sympathy for people. He especially liked older women. He felt they had been left alone and needed to be protected. It was a good thing because he became advisor-in-chief to all the old indigent widows in the town. They adored him because he looked after them.

"Would you like me to keep it safely?" he would ask when the Post Office savings book or pension book was produced out of a handbag.

In return he was rewarded on their death with yet another lustre jug or a Staffordshire ornament. Or a richly decorated cup and saucer with a caption saying it was a "Present" from somewhere or other — Portrush perhaps. Our house was full of them. I still have in my possession some of those treasures which have survived all those years, now much more valuable.

"It's one of your old ladies, Joe," my mother would joke him. But on the whole she approved of his kindness to these old women. She was a do-gooder herself in a small way.

But one day, Dad informed her matter-of-factly. "I've invited Mrs Nazer to come and stay with us."

My mother just looked at him. At last she said, "You've what?"

"I've invited a Mrs Nazer to come and stay. You may not know her."

My mother was speechless. "To — come and stay — here?"

"Yes, she can sleep in the visitor's room."

"But what's wrong with her own house?"

"She can't afford it. She's recently widowed you see."

My mother's hand went up worriedly to tidy her unruly hair. "When is she coming?"

"This afternoon."

My mother took that in. "Well, I'd better make her bed."

This was the limit. But what could mother do? The deed was done and the old lady's arrival imminent. There was no doubt Mumper was upset, but that did not prevent her from preparing a room and warmly welcoming the old girl when she arrived with all her wordly goods.

It was not long until we were quite used to seeing Mrs Nazer sitting in an armchair in the window of our dining room. She was a fixture, a frail creature covered in shawls. I was a fairly constant companion. She taught me to knit and the conversation flowed freely. I loved her dearly.

"Tell me a story, Mrs Nazer," I would say, sitting up on her knee.

"You can call me granny, pet," she said in a cultured English accent.

So I did. I loved her accent. It was so different from the usual harsh Northern Ireland accent and besides, I'd always wanted a granny. And this adopted one was exotic. She was alive and far better than my adopted grandfather — the portrait of Gladstone. She spoke, or told me stories about when she was young. Or read to me, beginning, "Once upon a time. . . ."

One day Mumper overheard me calling her granny.

"Don't you think that's silly?" she reasoned.

"No, I want a granny," I argued.

"But you know perfectly well, she's not your granny!"

I had to admit she wasn't. Although I grew up in an affectionate household, story-telling was frowned on. My mother had strict principles, but she always appealed to one's commonsense. There was no need to lay down hard and fast laws.

Mrs Nazer stayed on. There was no sign of her going. Although Mumper couldn't stop my father collecting stray ducks, she was determined they weren't to be full members of the family. At the time I thought it was harsh, but now I understand. So, while being awfully kind to Mrs Nazer, my mother's mind was made up — the old woman was not to eat with the family. Her food was served to her on a tray — always dainty and appetizing you may be sure — which she ate alone in the dining room.

"I'm sure Mrs Nazer must have relations," Mumper would mutter from time to time.

But my father wouldn't be budged. "She's all alone in the world. And a stranger in Ireland. We must be kind to her."

"You mean she's staying for ever?"

"Yes, Liz."

My parents didn't discuss Mrs Nazer anymore.

But I wasn't surprised when Mum announced, very casually, one evening at supper, "Well, thank goodness, I've been able to trace Mrs Nazer's married daughter."

My father looked surprised. "I didn't know she had a daughter."

"Oh, yes, she seems quite well off, lives in Harrogate."

My father paled. Slowly he put down his knife and fork.

"And what's more," Mum went on, "She'll be pleased to have her mother live with her."

My father was flabbergasted.

There was a silence.

We waited.

"What have you done, Liz?" he inquired quietly. "Did you consult Mrs Nazer?"

"Oh, yes," Mumper said lightly. "We've had quite a little chat about it. She'll be leaving us in about a week's time."

And that was that — my mother had won. Dad slept in the spare room that night and there were no further discussions about the matter — not in front of the children anyhow.

On the specified date, Mrs Nazer was all packed and ready to go. Mrs Hackett, her daughter, came to collect her. She was a very well dressed bossy, bosomy lady. Mumper and she didn't seem to have much in common.

"Are you ready, Mother?" Mrs Hackett boomed as if at an imbecile.

The old lady nodded from beneath her shawls.

There was no delay. It was a case of hail and farewell.

Dad stayed in the background and quickly disapppeared when the ladies had gone.

It took a little while before things returned to normal. Then, I suppose, Dad began to see that Mumper had acted for the best. At least, he hoped so.

But I had lost my one and only granny. It wasn't long before the letters started to arrive and they were all addresssed to me, "Darling, precious Muriel." They were read aloud at breakfast to the ribald remarks of my sisters, because I couldn't read her writing. "Precious Muriel," was my new name.

"Here comes precious Muriel," they chanted when I came and nobody stopped them.

I began to dread the sight of those letters. Then they stopped and one day Mrs Hackett wrote to say that her mother had passed away.

I was very sad.

"Where did she pass to?" my Dad wondered, putting down the letter. "Why can't she say *died* and have done with it."

He looked reproachfully at my mother. He didn't mince his words. "Poor old soul, died of loneliness and neglect, I suppose."

My mother left the room. But that was the end of my grandmother and no more old ladies appeared on my horizon.

13

"How would you girls like to go to a party?" Mumper said one evening. "A dance in fact?"

We gawped at her. A dance? She must be teasing.

Dancing was forbidden: it was a thing our parents were of one mind about. Time and time again, we had pleaded, cajoled, first one, then the other, to let us go to a dancing class. But the answer was always no, no, and a thousand times no. Collectively and singly there was no divergence. We finally saw the futility of mentioning the subject and resigned ourselves. Poor us, we thought, landed with such cruel parents who didn't want us to have any fun. I think this objection came mainly from my mother's Puritan background, but my father also had strong views on some things.

But now what was Mumper saying?

"I'm serious, " she said. "It's a fancy dress for children to be held in the Grand Hotel — in aid of the Lifeboat fund."

For once words failed us. When it did finally sink in our excitement knew no bounds. The Grand Hotel, we were going to a dance in the Grand Hotel. We had passed it so many times on our walks. In those days Bangor was one long street. We lived at the top of it, but if you turned right at the end you saw the Grand Hotel on the sea.

The place was magic. We had never been inside its portals as it wasn't a place our parents would ever frequent. But on this occasion the Rector's wife, who was on the organising committee of the Lifeboat Fund had "got at" our parents, convincing them there would be no harm in it. I don't know what arguments were used but, whatever they were, they worked. And the Rector's wife would be there in person to keep an eye on things and on us in particular.

The big question now was — how were we going to be dressed? There was no problem about Nan who was a born Kate Greenaway. But I was the awkward one. Books were studied and pictures looked at. Finally, to my horror, I was told I was going as a chrysanthemum.

"I'm not!" I argued. "I want to go like Nan."

"But you can't both be Kate Greenaways!"

It was hard not to be envious of Nan who was always so pretty. She always looked nice, no matter what she wore. Her dress had a high, almost regency waist-line, but she wore no pantaloons — my mother wouldn't have anything like that. I was shown the picture of a chrysanthemum and became reconciled to going as a flower. I had to stand on a chair in the kitchen while my costume was all sewn on me — orange sateen underneath and brown tulle on top.

It seemed ages, but the day came.

My fluffy dress was constructed on me and I wore a crown of tiny chrysanthemums in my hair, which was specially curled for the occasion. I had masses of reddish brown hair, but that was no use — Lady Godiva was an unlikely bet for a fancy dress. With shawls wrapped around our beautiful dresses, we stepped into our cab. It should have been a fairy coach. It was in a way, and the Grand Hotel was the sort of place Cinderella went to. I felt like her that night — except I had a beautiful sister instead of an ugly one.

The hotel was *en fete* for the occasion — to think we were actually going to a dance there. I'll never forget walking into that magical place with its balloons, fairy lights and musical band in the distance. The children were all very superior and outside our normal social world. The older boys stood around in Eton jackets — many of them went to a famous public school in the North of England. Some of the younger boys and girls were already there in fancy dress — everything from pirates to kings, from crinolined ladies to fairies. But there weren't any other chrysanthemums and people kept asking me what I was supposed to be.

"A chrysanthemum," I muttered, redfaced.

They didn't seem impressed.

The evening started with a grand parade past the judges because there were to be prizes for the best costumes. Nan and I walked in it nervously, but we didn't win anything. A boy dressed as a letter box got first prize for boys. And a mermaid got the girls' prize — her tail came off when the dancing started.

Although we'd never learnt to dance, we had hardly any difficulty. We did things like "The Grand Old Duke of York" and "Lancers" which was dead easy, and "The Grand Chain". Also the "Paul Jones" where you went round in a circle and had to rush to get someone you liked. Then we did Polkas, which were easy too — just one, two, three and a hop. Waltzes were the hardest. Then we had supper — jelly and cake, lemonade and buns, apple tart and delicious flans with lots and lots of cream and a fancy bag of sweets for everyone. It was the first wonderful evening in my whole life. High Society of the like I'd never seen before. I was drunk with the music, the lights and the laughter.

But Dad called for us before it was over. How could he?

"The cab is outside," he said, standing there hat in hand ready to go.

"But it's not over yet," I argued.

"Please, Daddy!" Nan pleaded.

"The cab is waiting, children."

You didn't argue with my father. If he said, go, you went. But it was with difficulty that a tired Kate Greenaway and a tattered chrysanthemum were prised away from all that magic. Reluctantly we followed him out to the horsedrawn cab. But as the horse clattered home, the music sounded in my head. There were no tears, but I think Dad was glad to hand us over to Mum.

"It was wonderful," I said dreamily.

Mumper listened to every word we had to tell and didn't

just bustle us off to bed until she thought we were ready. I must've looked sad, because she asked, "What's wrong, Muriel?"

"Nothing!"

"But you're looking sad — when you should be happy!"

"It's just over!"

After the ball is over, many a heart is aching — it's certainly true about life. But that wonderful evening had a good result: We were sent to a proper dancing class and a new and beautiful dimension was added to our lives.

14

About this time a new star came into our firmament — Auntie Onya. She was heralded by a strange man who appeared one day without warning on our roof garden. Nan and I had a favourite game which we played out there. There was a large tub of nasturtiums against one wall and this was the habitation of a colony of "Hairy Marys" — caterpillars in fact. Our game was to select two or more of the creatures and race them against each other, propelled and pushed by little sticks to keep them on the straight and narrow. It was very exciting.

"What's the betting?" a deep voice said behind us one day.

We looked up in surprise. The stranger in our yard had a stiff waxed moustache and a white waistcoat with a gold chain festooned across it, grey trousers and a black and white striped jacket. He looked like something out of a circus.

"Who are you?" I asked nervously. I'd been told never to talk to strangers.

He put an arm around each of us. "You can call me Jack. I'm your Auntie Onya's friend."

Our Auntie Onya's friend? But who was she? We didn't know of any aunties except Auntie Isobel in the country who was married to our funny uncle. We did, of course, have an auntie far away in America who sent Mumper lovely magazines with lovely recipes which she tried out. But the Jack person couldn't mean her.

He saw our surprise. "Well, never mind. Let's get on with your game. May I join in?"

We didn't particularly want him to, but there was no way out. So we politely collected three more "Hairy Marys" and put them on the race track.

"The one nearest the wall's yours," I instructed. "The next one's Nan's and this is mine. The first one to the fence wins."

To our surprise he dug into his pocket and gave us each a penny. Then he spread his clean hanky on the ground. "Now we'll all put our pennies together on my hanky — it'll be the kitty."

"What's that?" Nan asked suspiciously.

"It's where gamblers put their bets," he explained. "And whoever's "Hairy Mary" wins, gets the lot."

"The whole thruppence?" Nan was wide-eyed.

"It's called backing," he said, eyeing his caterpillar with disgust as it turned backward. "Give mine a prod there, Nan!"

I jumped up and down with excitement as my caterpillar crawled in front. I was winning, which made Nan whine a bit. She might have ended up in tears if Mumper had not arrived at that moment.

"Jack, what are you doing?" she chided, seeing the pennies on the hanky.

"We're backing." I prodded my fellow.

Mumper turning to the Jack person. "Don't put such notions into their head, Jack!"

He looked a bit shamefaced. "Ach, it'll do them no harm, Liz."

She was too late though. The excitement of watching my particular "Hairy Mary" cross the finishing line in front of the others that day had sown the seed. I became a gambler in a small way.

Then Mum explained who our Aunt was. "Onya's my eldest sister. She's come all the way from America. I haven't seen her for years. She's staying for awhile until she decides what to do. Dad's just gone down to the station to meet her."

The Jack person looked put out. "But I intended to meet her! Why didn't he tell me?"

There was no time to reply. At that moment the Aunt arrived and all was confusion and kissing and hugging and crying and laughing as Mumper greeted her long lost sister.

"Onya, dear, dear Onya! And these are my girls — Muriel and Nan. Children kiss your Auntie Onya!"

We did shyly. Helen was taking her nap.

"Call me Onya, children, not "Auntie" she said. "It makes me feel younger!"

We agreed to this. Really she didn't look like an Auntie at all. She wasn't a typical Northern Ireland woman but a bit exotic. She looked like Barbra Streisand and was small and beautifully dressed. I remember her smell above all, she always wore a nice perfume. Poor Mumper looked awfully old fashioned beside her, although she was much younger and prettier.

Everyone was crying and fussing, but at last they got themselves sorted out.

"Let's show you your bedroom!" Mum said, leading the way to the second best spare room. Dad and Jack followed with the luggage and, of course, we brought up the tail end. It was like a peep show as we all stood around watching her.

She swept off her hat. "Now, I think I need a nap! Will you all please vanish!"

We did — except Jack, who stayed behind.

Trailing back down stairs, we wondered what had hit us and asked Mumper, "But why didn't you tell us she was coming?"

"Because I didn't know for sure! Your Auntie Onya —"

"It's Onya!" Nan insisted.

"Oh, Onya then," Mumper went on. "Onya's very unpredictable. I never know if she's coming or going. Her head is always full of great ideas!"

"You're telling me!" Dad muttered grimly, but his vein was throbbing.

Naturally we bombarded them with more questions which they couldn't or wouldn't answer – although, there was no hint of disapproval of Onya and Jack's unusual friendship.

"I'm just as surprised as you," Mumper went on. "You

see, I thought Onya had gone to America for good. It's very far away, children, and sometimes people never come back."

I thought of our wild uncles and the empty schoolroom in poor Uncle Joseph's country house. They had never come back.

"But who's the Jack person?" I asked.

"Oh he — he's a friend from my part of the country." Mumper tucked up a stray lock of hair. She did this when she was embarrassed.

"Is he staying too?"

"No!" Dad said emphatically.

"But then what's he doing in her bedroom?"

Dad didn't answer but his vein throbbed again. And Mumper went off, bent on hospitality, to make a celebration supper.

It seemed a very long time before Onya and Jack re-appeared from their nap. In fact supper was waiting and so were we. It was a noisy meal, during which we ate the fatted calf for the prodigal's return and everybody talked and laughed too much.

At last Dad looked at his watch. "Time for your train, Jack."

Jack consulted his own watch at the end of that long gold chain strung across his fancy waistcoat. "By Jove, yes! I'll just make the last train if I hurry."

Apparently he lived in Belfast.

"Well, I'll be off, so!" He stood up, tweaking his moustache and clearing his throat and looking around in suprise, hoping someone would detain him.

But nobody did.

Onya stayed with us for a few weeks and was visited frequently by Jack. I brought up her breakfast on a tray and loved nothing better than to sit on her bed while she told stories of her and Mumper's youth on the farm in Tyrone. But otherwise her visit didn't affect us — we went to school as usual, played as usual, had our meals as usual. All the same, after a time we wished she'd go. She took up too much of Mum's time and it wasn't the same when she was there.

But at last the day came when she moved off, bag and baggage. And what a lot there was — suitcases, trunks, hat boxes of every size and shape.

"She and a lady called Miss Earley are going to open a select hat salon in Belfast," Mumper said. "Jack's going to be a shareholder."

We wondered what a shareholder was.

"It means he's investing money in the business. They're all going to live together in a house in Belfast," she went on.

Dad cleared his throat, muttering behind his paper. "I hope it works out."

But he looked doubtful.

And that's just what they did. The three of them found a little three storey building — it must've been in either Anne Street or Cornmarket — and a house in Botanic Avenue. Miss Earley was a tall dark American lady, the very opposite to Onya. Although she was lovely in a different way, I remember we didn't like her. Mum took Nan and me to the hat shop opening and we thought it a bit queer that there was only one hat in the window and a lot of tulle and chiffon and artificial flowers. Still it was a lovely hat. Inside there were more hats on stands, but no counter, which we thought rather odd for a shop.

"But it's a salon," we were told firmly. "Not a shop."

On the next floor there was just one room — the work-room. Here four or five girls sat around a table, snipping and sewing and making lovely hats. They made bonnets for Nan and me while we were there with rosettes at the side and great big bows. Jack was in the workroom, talking to the girls.

On the next floor there was a sort of kitchen–cum–sitting room in which we had tea and buns. It was all very exciting, but soon the time came to go. It always seemed time to go when you were enjoying yourself. Jack hailed a cab and we drove back to the station in style.

"Thank goodness that's over!" Mum sighed with relief as the train moved off. "I hope it will last."

But she sounded doubtful.

When we got home our bonnets were taken away and we were never allowed to wear them. Mother was much too practical and we moved in a different strata of society to Onya.

"But can't I wear my bonnet?" I would argue.

"No," Mum said.

"But why?"

"It's not practical."

And that was that.

Initially, the hat salon was a complete success. Rich Belfast ladies vied with each other to have a Booth, Earley hat. Only the very well-off could afford them, of course, but they became the visible sign of a comfortable bank balance. No wedding was considered complete without one. "Tuppence halfpenny looking down on tuppence," Mum snapped scornfully. But I think in her heart of hearts, she was the greatest snob of all. Not that she would have put it like that. But like most Ulster landed people she had this feeling of superiority. It was ridiculous really.

Alas, the hat salon didn't last. Apparently the threesome wasn't a good idea. I expected Dad to say, "I told you so." But he refrained. The domestic arrangements, we were told, were not satisfactory. We children were consumed with curiosity, but had to be content with being told that Onya and Jack had gone to Dublin and bought a big house on the seafront in Bray — a hotel now, I've no doubt. Miss Earley, we were told, had returned to America. It all seemed mysterious and exciting to us. "Shocking" was the word Mum used.

"But why?" we would ask.

But then she'd just take a fit of the giggles and sing,

> "How happy would I be with either
> Were other dear charmer away."

94

Although there was no question of my parents being shocked, I suppose a *ménage-à-trois* was outrageous in those days. Or maybe I should say *avant-garde*. Although the same things went on as today, they were covered up more. People observed the proprieties. Appearances were everything. It was all very hypocritical. Onya must have been a bit of a flyer. Mum said she seemed pleased with herself for winning Jack and hoped pride didn't go before a fall. And anyway, one man, Jack, would not do for two ladies. But Jack, conceited and cocksure man that he was, apparently thought differently. Because within a year or so he deserted Onya to chase Miss Earley to America. She was wiser and insisted on marriage or nothing, or was she?

"Early bird catches the worm," Mum joked.

And we thought that, after all, Jack was a sort of worm. He had even played with them. Anyway it was the last we ever heard of them.

Onya, of course, was always with us, figuratively anyway. Her heart was not broken by Jack. Over the years, rumours reached us of other entanglements. She eventually married and bought a house in Bangor, but she was respectable by that time. She sent Dad two pairs of hand-knitted socks every Christmas and wrote him long epistles which he loved getting. She had a colourful way of writing. She was in Dublin at the time of the 1916 Rising and sent him a "garbled" account of it — he said — but I wish I had that letter now. Onya could have made anything into an arresting story. I suppose it was how she saw life. Anyway we always looked forward to her letters which arrived at irregular intervals, and to hearing Dad chuckle over them.

15

After our final trip to Co Tyrone, we had no holidays for several years. Bangor, with all the amenities of a popular seaside town, offered entertainment enough. While my sisters loved bathing, I hated it. I far preferred tennis and, later on, golf. Still, I dutifully went to the Ladies' Bathing Place almost every morning. It was situated at a discreet distance from the men's. "Never the twain shall meet" was the rule. Even then, the swimming pool was hidden from public view by a steep bank, but the usual amenities were inside and several attendants to keep an eye on our safety. I always sat on the edge of the pool, dabbling my toes, until someone pushed me in. But Nan was the continual show-off and eyecatcher. She could dive and do everything like that and thoroughly enjoyed it. Helen was still small and splashed about in the shallow end sustained by water wings.

Most of all we envied all the lucky people who went to Lenaghan's jetty and hired rowing boats. Captain Lenaghan was an "old salt" or pretended to be. He wore a navy blue reefer jacket with brass buttons and a peaked nautical cap. He had a dozen or more boats for hire.

"Can we go in a boat, Dad," I begged.

He took us out once or twice, but wasn't much good. Mum, of course, wouldn't set foot in a boat.

We must've kept on begging, because one day we were taken down to the jetty.

"Captain Lenaghan has a boat for you, and he's going to give you lessons," Dad announced.

Oh, joy!

The boat was a light skiff called *The Mary Ann*. She was

lovely and we were duly taken out for our first lesson. Captain Lenaghan taught us how to put the oars into the rowlocks, how to steer and, above all, to row. Nan took to it immediately, while Helen was a non-starter. Although I never learned to feather my oars, I improved in time, and became quite capable of taking the Mary Anne out by myself — as long as the sea was calm. It was lovely to drop anchor a short distance from the shore and loll in the bottom of the boat reading. I read for hours sometimes, until a loud shout came from the shore, "Ahoy there!"

I wasn't the Captain's favourite.

The evening's entertainment was S G Montgomery's open air gospel meetings. They were held on a permanent site just above the jetty, with a little covered platform and unmovable seats. People gathered there on summer evenings. Mostly, everybody stood because of the Collection Box. If you were sitting, there was no escape when it was rattled under your nose, but if standing you could move away. It was mostly singing, accompanied by a small portable organ. I loved to join the townspeople in singing things like,

> Shall we gather at the river,
> (at the river)
> The beautiful, the beautiful river.
> (river)
> Gather with the saints at the river
> (at the river)
> That flows by the throne of God!

There were others and we knew them all. But we weren't really encouraged to go there. Dad was firmly Church of Ireland and Mum probably thought the people common. But I loved it, and they must've agreed that we wouldn't come to any harm mentally or physically.

The other thing I remember about Montgomery's was their large drapery store. We thought it the last word in elegance, especially at Christmas, when evening dresses were displayed. It was Nan's and my ambition to get decked out in one — utterly unrealistic, of course, in our uneventful life. But we argued for hours about who would get which dress.

One evening I was sent on some errand which took me past the laundry. A huge tent was erected on the spare space in front and a sign said, "Revivalist Meeting."

What was that? People were going in and I had lots of time. But should I?

I stood there for awhile then cautiously edged my way in, pushing right up to the front with the other youngsters. The tent was hot and very packed. There was a hush as the "Hot Gospeller" appeared on the platform.

He was a popular Welsh evangelist, I found out later. A big fat man in a black suit. That day I watched with awe as he worked everybody up into a frenzy of excitement.

I can see him now, exhorting the audience about the wickedness of their ways. If they didn't repent, they couldn't live with God. They had to be saved.

"Come and be washed in the blood of the Lord," he shouted.

"Praise, the Lord!" they shouted back over and over again.

I joined in.

"Hallelujah!"

It got louder and louder. "Hallelujah!"

People began stamping their feet and soon everybody was all over the place.

"Do you repent of your sins?" the preacher called in ringing tones.

"Yes!" we shouted back. "Yes!"

Then, at the crescendo of excitement, he announced in a low voice, "The collection will now be taken."

The collection? I had a penny so I put it in. Then the noise started all over again. It was infectious and I was carried away again by the desire to repent and be born anew.

"Will those who repent and want to be saved come

forward to the front!" he shouted.

People walked up. Wanting to be saved, I followed.

Then I must've passed out or something, because I don't know what happened next. I came to in the open air. It was late, I noticed, and ran all the way home where tea was nearly over.

Dad glared at me. "Where have you been?"

When I told him, he looked about to hit me.

But he thumped the table instead, his blue eyes flashing, "Don't ever, ever in all your life, put your foot in a place like that again!"

I gaped at him, afraid to say I was saved.

"They are evil, do you hear me?"

"Yes, Dad."

"Evil!" He thumped the table again. "You have your own church to go to!"

I'd never seen him so cross before.

"Do you hear me?"

I was so scared, I jumped off my chair and went up to my bedroom. I threw myself on my bed, shaking and sobbing my heart out. I was saved, but nobody cared. I wept and wept. It seemed like the end of the world. I'd run away. To America, like all my uncles. Instead I must've fallen asleep.

A slight touch on my shouler awakened me. Mum was there with a large slice of apple tart.

"It's all over," she said kindly.

I muttered that I was sorry.

"Just a bad mistake, pet. Anybody can make mistakes."

"Even Dad?" I asked shakily.

"Even Dad."

And that was that. But it seemed a long time before Dad and I were really pally. It was probably my fault. I think I was afraid he might erupt again. One thing is sure: I never went to another Revivalist Meeting, not even Dr Billy Graham years later. But maybe I didn't need to — after all, I'd been saved once.

The holidays ended and school started again. One afternoon, I arrived home and Mum said casually, "Get my sewing
box in the drawing room, Muriel."

I obeyed.

It was just inside the door: a piano.

I couldn't believe my eyes. I went over and touched it to
make sure it was real.

"Mum! Mum!" I shouted. "Come and see!"

She came and hugged me. It was rosewood and trimmed
with dark green silk, its keys were ivory coloured, not white.
It was so beautiful I nearly cried. I touched the keys timidly
and the sound that came out was like fairy music, sort of tinkly,
but it was out of tune. My sure ear told me.

"Never mind, a piano tuner can fix that!" Mum assured
me.

I touched the keys again, lovingly, hoping she was right.

"This was your Dad's idea," she said gently.

My heart gave a great leap. All was forgiven and forgotten.

"Is it mine?" I asked.

"No, it's for all of you."

But that did not diminish its value. I knew I'd enjoy it the
most.

The piano tuner came the next day. He was a cross little
man who wouldn't let me stay and watch. He took ages, but,
after he left, the piano was perfect. It was situated exactly under
a large picture of our maternal grandmother. She was beautiful
like Queen Victoria, but far prettier. She wore the usual lace
cap and a lace shawl round her shoulders and her beautiful
hands were reposing peacefully on an expansive lap. She had
a tiny smile on her sweet face as she looked down on her
grand-daughter. We really had something in common. As I
played, I thought of her beautiful wild garden and finding
Brother Anthony's grave. We couldn't go to the country any
more, but it was just as good to think about it. It's funny, but
I'd never looked at that picture before the piano was placed
under it. So I got to know her very well.

Next we had to find a suitable music teacher, preferably one who would come to our house and take us all. Money was always important in our family, but at last we found someone — Mrs Ritchie, a spinster of indeterminate age and a regular communicant at our church. She was small and skinny with a rosy face. Although she was never cross, my doubts grew as to her ability as a musician. But she could play hymns beautifully and talked a lot. We all soon loved her. Mum always gave her a cup of tea before she started on me. I was the last and most difficult. Maybe I asked too many questions in my eagerness to learn. But I couldn't help it, it was a magic thing to me. The other two didn't care anyway. To them she was just a necessary evil — something to get through.

We had other lessons besides the piano. About this time Mum was worried that we were acquiring the local accent, so a specialist had to be consulted. In this case an elocution teacher called Miss O'Neill. We were despatched to her house once a week, which we didn't like much. We had to go up a long, long narow dark path bordered with laurels and it always seemed to be raining. Also we had to bring slippers with us, so as not to destroy her carpets with muddy feet. Once there, we shed our sodden coats and shoes in what had been a conservatory and then crept like mice into a warm firelit sitting room to endure further torture in the company of half-a-dozen or so other unfortunates.

The first exercise was voice production, vowels in particular.

"Say O," Miss O'Neill instructed us.

"O," we parroted.

"Ah."

"Ah."

"A."

"A."

Although I've never forgotten my vowels, the class wasn't fun. But we pupils had a fellow feeling for each other. We had to learn the most ridiculous things — how to stand properly. How to sit like ladies. Then — and this was the funniest — how to use our hands gracefully with the two middle fingers slightly bent and a gracious turn of the wrist. I still find myself doing this — it was something like being taught an Eastern dance. Finally came the job of memorising "pieces." My favourite was the *Bald headed Man*. Because it wasn't verse, I could improvise if I forgot the odd word or two. It was about the adventures of this poor man and an annoying fly. The Christmas play was *Scrooge*.

A lesson I really enjoyed was singing. For this my mother employed the services of a very well known singer, Madame Daisy Creaney. This was her professional name. She was really called Mrs Rogers and was a small fat lady with a tremendous voice who taught us to sing the scales, mostly, up and down, high and low — Do, re, me, fa, soh, la, ti, do. There were two other girls in the class — Dorothy, her daughter, and Flossie Campbell who later married well and became the mother of a famous Belfast actor. Eventually we became known as the "three little maids from school" as we were called on to sing that song from *The Mikado* at all the local concerts, dressed in Kimonos of course.

But I enjoyed anything to do with music.

"I want you to look for your old boots in the box room," Mum said one day. "Someone might be able to wear them."

The box room had neither rhyme nor reason to it, so this was a herculean task. Things were just thrown in, higgeldy-piggeldy. But I got round to looking for the boots.

They were nowhere to be seen.

I pulled things out, making the mess even worse, my temper keeping pace with my frustration. Where were my boots? Then my eye caught a unfamiliar box. It was heavy but I hauled it out and took the lid off.

It was full of music.

Excitedly I got down on my hunkers and looked through

my treasure trove. What a find — everything from five finger exercises to the classics, from popular songs to, oh joy, a big bound book of Irish songs. I flicked through this. They were mostly traditional, and some rebel.

Time was forgotten.

"Have you got lost, Muriel?" Mum called at last.

I emerged hot and dusty, without the boots. "Come and see what I've found!"

She didn't seem surprised, but helped me carry the contents out bit by bit — the box was too heavy to lift.

"Goodness," she said, "I wonder where this came from?"

Was she surprised or only pretending? Dad was no better.

"Take it as a gift from the Gods," was all he said without looking up from his paper.

With hindsight, it was probably a job lot at a sale which they'd bought years ago. It was quite a conglomeration and quite higgeldy-piggeldy, but provided hours and hours of pure joy.

Time and fate wait for no man and we were getting old enough to know that there were strange things going on in our midst. All was not peace and tranquility. Home Rule was at the bottom of it and Ulster would have none of it. A new name was on everyone's lips — Sir Edward Carson, a Dubliner and a barrister. There were meetings everywhere and when he was to speak, the response was phenomenal.

The South was in turmoil too. Onya wrote about a man called Larkin who was rallying the ill-paid workers. He was no respecter of persons and his ire was said to be directed particularly at the "ould hussy up in the Park." That was Lady Aberdeen, the Lord Lieutenant's wife. So what with Home Rule, Rome Rule, Mr Larkin, and Mr de Valera, Sir Edward Carson, Sir James Craig and Galloper Smith, who became the great Lord Birkenhead, things were in a mess. We weren't greatly concerned, but took in more than anybody realized.

At this time, a lot of people, mostly retired with relatives in the North, began to percolate into our part of the world. Among them were our relatives from Co Tipperary, Mr and Mrs Culpepper who seemed quite old to us. He was a retired professor or school teacher or something of that ilk. They acquired a terraced house in a road not far away from us and my Mum thought he surely would be glad to instruct her daughters in the rudiments of literature in which she believed we were almost totally illiterate. And so, to our sorrow, it was arranged twice weekly.

It was a horrible house, cold and dark with a funny smell. Mr Culpepper was tall and stooped with a very red face and white hair and nose with a continual drip. I don't think he liked little girls, although he had two or three daughters.

"Good morning, girls," he said gruffly in a strange accent. "We'll begin our studies with the Book of Common Prayer." He held up the prayer book. "Are you familiar with it?"

We nodded. We sat at a table in a small room behind the front door. It had linoleum on the floor and I wondered if the smell came from that. It was a stale, sort of dirty smell.

"It is very fine literature, the finest."

He went on agonisingly in this vein for a few weeks. Then we graduated to the classics. He was so boring, I can't remember what or which, although I loved literature. I'm sure we were nothing but an annoyance to the poor man, because one day in an attempt to rouse us from our lethargy, he gave us a rendering of *The Raven* by Edgar Allan Poe. He recited it vigorously, his white hair wild, but that gloomy lament for the lost Lenore with its endless "Nevermores" did little to cheer us up.

16

When Mum got restless, we knew it was holiday time again. She really believed it wasn't good for people to be cooped up too long in the same place. And now that we didn't go to the country, something had to be planned. Something that everybody would enjoy.

Of all places, they chose Toomebridge on the River Bann.

"There's an old country house for rent," Mum said enthusiastically. "With a big garden. It's near the River Bann where you can all fish."

It seemed ideal. Dad especially was a very keen fisherman and knew the owner of the Salmon and Eel Fishing Company which operated from Toomebridge. So the big black trunk was pulled out of the box room and preparations began.

Mum was excited. "It'll be a quiet holiday," she kept saying. "So don't bring much. We're only staying a month."

But nobody took much interest. Somehow it wasn't the same as going to Co Tyrone. I don't even remember how we got there, just that it was raining. But I do remember the house.

I'm sure the sight of it made Mum's stout heart fail. It was big and dilapidated, with just the bare necessities. The bedrooms were large, but there was nothing wrong with the beds. The kitchen was vast and the cooking arrangements primitive. The dining room was a day's march from the kitchen, so we decided to live and eat there.

"We'll be out so much, it won't matter! We can have picnics in the grounds!"

Our Mum was a great optimist. We were competely cut off from humanity by the large overgrown grounds and some way from the little town of Toomebridge. It took a day to find our bearings and get accustomed to the barracks of a house. But strange to say, it wasn't eerie and we developed a kind of liking for it. The river wasn't very far away and it was wide and deep. An old Captain and his wife lived on the other side and we could see his house. It was very long and low and white, quite large and cosy-looking. We envied him and his wife. But it wasn't long before they established contact with us. They left a boat for Dad and an invitation for us all to have supper with them.

They were nice people but seemed ancient to us, older even than Mum and Dad. Strangely, I remember what we had for supper — hot salmon and white sauce. The Captain arranged that on good days he'd send a boat for us children with a boy to row and look after us. Down river was Church Island, and upriver was Toomebridge.

And so a pattern was established. Dad fished constantly and had a great time. He caught no salmon, but some trout which Mum cooked. It tasted quite different from the fish you buy in a shop. As we knew how to row, we were allowed to go in our boat ourselves. But it was flat bottomed which made it harder to steer. We felt proud that we could get it under the Bridge, but preferred Church Island. We found a company of Boy Scouts camping there. They tolerated us, but only just — girls. And too young at that.

The whole place was creepy, in a way. And although the weather was gorgeous, I don't think Mum liked it too much. She was soon counting the days till she could get home.

"I'm tired of the river always running the same way!" she complained dottily.

If just once, by some miracle, it could have gone the other way, it might've lessened the monotony. But it didn't. She would not go fishing with Dad and was uneasy about us in a boat by ourselves. So she began to tidy the garden, but that was a lost cause. Her only consolation was that Dad was enjoying it. Then help came by way of the local vicar's wife who had a little pony and trap and was probably in just as much need of company.

One evening towards the end of our month's exile, Dad came in with his usual fish and usual appetite.

"That fellow de Valera is coming to Castledawson tomorrow, speaking if you please," he said halfway through Mum's delicious meal. "I'm thinking of going. What about it, Liz?"

Mum put down her fork. "I wouldn't listen to that fellow if you paid me. And I don't know what would take you, Joe."

Dad finished his plate, saying, "We're going to hear more of that young man. Even if he's a troublemaker, we mightn't get the chance to see him again."

"Well, you go, dear. But don't expect me to."

"I don't. But no harm in asking, is there?" Then he turned to me. "What about you, Muriel? Would you like to go?"

"Yes!" Would I like to go? Of course, I would. I listened to everything, so had heard that man's name mentioned often. He lived far away in Dublin. But I had no interest in him. I was only interested in going off with my Dad for the day.

"Well, that's settled then," he said, looking anxiously at Mum. "If your mother agrees. We'll have to make an early start. Maybe a few sandwiches would come in handy, Liz?"

Mum started clearing the table. "Of course, Joe. Would you like champagne to go with them?"

I knew she wasn't pleased. But was she annoyed with Dad, or de Valera, or me?

"Off to bed, then," said Dad. "It's Shank's pony tomorrow!"

Tomorrow I'm going to Castledawson, I thought, going to sleep. Castledawson, and we'll be walking all the way. But it's not all that far.

The next morning we'd just started our long walk when the local doctor stopped in his pony and trap. "I suppose you're going to the meeting?"

My Dad said yes.

"Jump in and I'll give you a lift."

We did and he went on talking. "I'm going to see patients myself. That fellow's a trouble maker."

"No harm in listening to what he has to say."

"Good luck to him, but I haven't the time. Nor the inclination." The doctor looked curiously at my Dad. "What brings you?"

"We're on holiday."

"Ah, nothing better to do!"

What did he mean? I was glad when he dropped us before we reached Castledawson. Did he not approve of Dad going to see this man with the funny name? But my father had a sense of history that was utterly unbiased.

There were crowds and crowds on the road and dozens of horse drawn vehicles, all heading for the town. The meeting was in the Square which was already crammed full of more horses and carts and traps and country people. The horses gave off a country smell, reminding me of Tyrone. And there were redfaced men, dressed in black and smelling of whiskey but not many women.

We pushed our way in.

"Like a seat in the front row?" a burly farmer asked.

"Thanks," Dad said and we climbed into his trap.

We had an excellent view from there. There was a band and lots of flags and noise. Everybody cheered and clapped as a figure climbed up on the back of a cart.

They say first impressions last and it's true. We were quite close, so I had a good view. Mr de Valera was tall and thin and young with a beaky nose and specs. He reminded me of a bird of prey, predatory like a vulture. His long thin arms were like wings, flapping in the breeze, and strangest of all, he wore a plaid blanket over one shoulder. A strange apparition to one small girl who couldn't make out a word he said. He certainly didn't look like the enthusiastic Irish around him, who were predominantly Roman Catholic, I later learnt. But then he wasn't really Irish, only a pretend one. At any rate, he wasn't a good speaker and quickly bored me. So, I studied the people around me.

Dad seemed to be bored too. "I think we'd better be going."

So we struggled back through the crowd.

"I didn't think much of that fellow," Dad said, or words to that effect.

We walked out of the town past a row of labourers' cottages with gardens in front. These were very neat and orderly and full of cabbages, lettuces, scallions and potatoes.

"I wonder would they sell any of the vegetables," Dad said. "Let's ask, shall we? Mum would love some."

So we opened the gate and walked down the garden path. The door of the house opened and out stepped a comely young woman with black curly hair, red cheeks and a clean white apron.

"Good day, Ma'am." Dad lifted his hat. "Lovely weather."

She smiled a wonderful smile. "Indeed it is, sir."

"I wonder if you'd be willing to sell some of your beautiful vegetables? My wife would love some."

"Certainly. Come into the kitchen."

It was very clean and a big pot was boiling on the peat fire.

"I'm just making my man's supper," she said. "It's champ. Would the little girl like some?"

"She would," my father said.

And so I was served with a bowl of mashed potatoes with lots of butter and chopped chives. I was given an iron spoon to eat it with. It was all very new to me and very delicious. She gave Dad a cup of tea and then they went into the garden to choose the vegetables. She gave him lots and lots of stuff, all for free, to Dad's embarrassment. But I saw him giving money to a small boy who appeared on the scene.

A curtain comes down on that scene so vividly remembered. All I know is that it was nicer than hearing Mr de Valera. Also for the first time, I saw my father as a man and someone other than my Dad. I'll never forget the look that country woman gave him as she said goodbye. And I'll never forget the twinkle in his eye. Someone must have given us a lift home that evening, but the rest of the holiday is in oblivion.

17

And so, back to home and school. Although trouble was brewing far away in the Baltics and nearer still in our own country, all was peaceful on our particular front. Dad was more than ever concerned with the church and church matters.

The time had come for my Confirmation. That event and its preparation classes were a very solemn and serious thing indeed. So serious that Dad caught a sort of religous bug.

"Be five minutes early for breafast in the morning," he informed us one evening.

We just looked at him. Why?

He cleared his throat awkwardly. "We're going to have morning prayers."

"Morning prayers?" I looked at Nan.

She giggled and Helen made a face. Mum started clearing the table. I knew by her look that she thought Dad was touched.

But the next morning found the three of us kneeling on the hard floor at the hard kitchen chairs while Dad read the collect for the day in a deadly serious voice. "Almighty God, who through thy only begotten Son, Jesus Christ, hast overcome death and opened unto us the gate of everlasting life. . . ."

It was enough to make a cat laugh and we were no better. I don't know who started it, but the three of us were in convulsions of laughter.

Dad glared, but the vein in his forehead was throbbing as he launched into the Lord's prayer. "Our Father, which art in Heaven. . . ."

I nearly choked.

This charade went on for about a week. Then Dad joined in the laughing himself. What a relief. I don't think he was cut out for the priestly role.

But I still had to cope with confirmation. I went all goody-goody and caught a religious bug myself. What puzzled me more than anything was the reiteration, in class after preparation class, of the desperate seriousness of ever, ever contemplating marrying a Roman Catholic. The puzzle remains with me to this day. Even if we were to end up old maids, and there was no worse fate in those days, it was to be avoided at all costs. But what if I fell in love with a Catholic? What would happen to me then?

I confided my fears in Dad.

"Ach, don't worry," he said. "We'll cross that bridge if it's ever necessary."

My Dad was so free of prejudice — if only there were more like him. But there weren't in those classes. We were taught meticulously, word by painful word, the differences in our churches — which don't seem to amount to anything today.

So the day came when the Bishop laid his hand on my head. I was now laden with new responsibilities and a desire to be really holy. I 'm sure I was an impossible little prig. And to complicate things, I fell helplessly in love.

It happened in church.

I looked up and there he was, sitting in a pew at right angles to ours. I could almost touch him, but only gazed. He was so beautiful, an angel, tall dark and handsome. But would he even look at someone so much younger?

I did everything to attract his attention. I sang my heart out. But he didn't even look in my direction.

The same thing happened next Sunday. And the Sunday after that. I learnt that he was called St Clair Barrett, and home from boarding school in the North of England. But there was no way we could meet as we moved in very different worlds. All I could do was gaze at his beautiful profile, with a funny feeling in the pit of my stomach.

Then one awful Sunday he wasn't there.

"Where's St Clair?" I asked my father casually.

"Oh, he's gone back to school."

It was all over. Love, forever unrequited.

But other things occupied my attention. One night in 1912, I was awakened and an eiderdown was thrown round me.

Dad whispered, "I want you to see something, Muriel."

I was guided in the darkness to the upstairs landing window. It was the middle of the night, yet a continuous stream of vehicles, nose-to-tail, was speeding past our house into the darkness beyond. There were hundreds and hundreds of them, every kind of vehicle from private cars to vans and lorries. There wasn't a soul in sight, nothing but this endless procession.

"What are they doing?" I asked.

"Shh! Gun-running," Dad whispered. Then he explained to me what that was. "It's strictly against the law, and yet all those men are bringing guns into the country. To all parts of Ulster. Look at them speeding into the darkness with their illegal loads." He sighed sadly.

"But what for?" I asked.

"To protect themselves and Ulster."

It was all very confusing. "But where are the police?"

Dad grinned. "All locked up. "There's a man at our front door who won't let me out. Nobody's allowed out tonight."

"That's funny."

"It's not funny, it's history."

"History?"

"Yes, I wanted you to see it with your own eyes."

And then I was bundled back to bed.

It gave me a funny feeling. I knew that all the young men and boys had been training for months, just like soldiers. And they had real soldiers to teach them. But now, they had real guns and ammunition too. What next? Would there be war in our own country?

Then we heard about the enormous meeting in Belfast. Thousands and thousands of men came to the City Hall to sign the Covenant. I wasn't sure then what the Covenant was. But it had something to do with No Home Rule and loyalty to King and Country, and that meant King George V in London. Some of the Covenanters were meant to have signed in their own blood, which was creepy. And all over Ulster, in every town and village, people took pledges to be true.

After all that the British Government decided to enforce their will and introduce Home Rule. A British regiment stationed at the Curragh, near Dublin, was ordered to march on Ulster and subdue this rebellious people. Carson's army was ready to repel them. But the British mutinied, I was told, and so avoided bloodshed. It was thrilling.

18

But the English had more than Ireland to think about. War clouds were gathering in Europe and Kaiser Bill was the new name on everybody's lips. Newspapers were the ordinary way of learning what was going on in the world outside Ireland, outside Ulster, outside Bangor. *The Evening Telegraph*, our only evening paper, had to come to Bangor by rail. The last edition, the eighth, as it was called, was delivered about eight o'clock and poor "Jeemes" Warden in his paper shop was mobbed. The papers were torn from him by a news-hungry crowd and the lucky emerged from the scrum un-scathed. We children were sent once or twice and returned empty-handed and frightened after being nearly trampled to death in the stampede. People really were news crazy and no wonder. All the world was balanced on a knife's edge.

Then in 1914, the German army invaded Belgium and Great Britain declared a "state of emergency." People went crazy. Even in Bangor there was rejoicing. They'd teach the Germans a lesson. Give Kaiser Bill a bloody nose and serve him jolly well right.

All the boys and men in the shops and stores and farm houses all over Ulster enlisted. They had formed Carson's Army and were more than half trained already at Clandeboye. They knew how to handle a gun and lob a grenade. They knew such a lot, or thought they did. Youth and enthusiasm were the key words. The cities, towns and villages of Ulster were bereft but proud. Many young men enlisted from the south too, but they had their own regiments and were not part of the great Ulster contingent. We children were taken to Belfast to see them off.

History again — our Dad was really a glutton for it.

Even to this day I can see them: the young and the brave, the short and the tall, the plain and the handsome, the rich man's son and the farm labourer, all marching together. A happy, happy band of brothers, thousands and thousands of them. I can hear the bands. I can see the flags. I remember the windows along the route packed with people and flags and more flags.

We were standing on the pavement, children in front. The soldiers must've been given the freedom of the city or something, because I could swear there were bayonets. But they were all laughing and waving to people, cocky and funny and singing, "It's a long, long way to Tipperary, it's a long way to go. . . ."

We cheered and laughed and waved too. It was a great, brave, wonderful send-off, although some women were crying behind the waving hankerchiefs. The YCV's they were called — Young Citizens' Volunteers. Later they would be amalgamated with all the other Ulster regiments into the Ulster Brigade, a proud name.

The docks were crowded. More bands played and flags waved. There was a mighty send-off as the soldiers crowded to the rails of the ships for last sight of those dirty docks. Then out through the channel to Belfast Lough and away. What were those merry, laughing, waving boys thinking? Would we see them again? Three quarters never came back.

19

The next day, we had the cold realities of school. The War was to change things drastically, but in Bangor change came slowly. We heard an army camp was to be opened at Clandeboye, just outside Bangor, and gradually more and more soldiers appeared on our streets. They wore ill-fitting coarse khaki uniforms and puttees and ugly clog-like army boots. They were recruits and mostly English — pale faced, thin boys — certainly not prepossessing. But, as is their way, the Ulster people were kind to them and took them into their homes. After all, they were somebody's sons away from home for the first time.

The Churches decided the recruits needed a club. A place where they could play games and eat cheaply, write letters and so on, strictly teetotal, of course. Dozens of volunteers were needed to run the place. Someone suggested to Mum that I was old enough to wash dishes. At first she objected. Young girls then were never allowed out alone, especially in the evening. But there was a war on. Finally, on the understanding that I had no contact with soldiers, I was allowed to go two evenings a week for a few hours.

I was thrilled. It was better than knitting. Everybody was knitting socks for soldiers. My contribution was a scarf, but it was now about two yards long and far from straight. It went in and out like the tide.

Someone called for me the first evening. But when we opened the door of the club, a cloud of smoke nearly blew us out again. Woodbines, I was told. It was almost solid smoke inside and we choked and spluttered. But you can get used to anything. The day came when I hardly noticed it. Washing dishes, endless coarse white dishes is not a thing to inspire one. I've never read a sonnet to a dishwasher — no wonder they invented automatic ones. Of course boredom set in, and one evening I wandered into the forbidden territory of the main hall.

It was packed with smoking soldiers. Also there was a stink. Maybe it was the khaki, or maybe soldiers were not so clean then. But the smell was awful — the more smoke the better. The poor things were trying to enjoy themselves. Some played tiddliwinks, some wrote letters, some played cards or ping-pong, or some just sat.

Then someone went to the piano and a sing-song started. "Pack up your troubles in your old kit bag and smile, smile, smile. . . ."

"Come on over, love," one of soldiers called.

But I hugged the wall.

Then they sang, "Tipperary. . . ."

I sang along with the boys.

"There's a concert next week," one of the helpers said later and I decided to be there.

Luckily the concert coincided with one of my dishwashing evenings, so it was easy to slip into a seat at the back. It was a variety concert, but not up to much, I thought. Still, it seemed to please the audience, judging by the applause. Towards the end there were loud calls for the Sergeant Major, who seemed unwilling to appear. But, finally, to ever increasing applause, a huge Sergeant Major made his slow way to the platform. Evidently he was an old favourite.

"The Tavern!" the boys shouted, stamping and whistling.

He cupped a hand over his ear. "I can't hear you!"

"The Tavern!"

More screams and whistles and stamping.

He looked puzzled. "What are they saying?"

"The Tavern!"

I was nearly deafened by the noise.

"The Tavern!"

Finally, the Sergeant signalled to the pianist and began in a deep, loud voice, "There's a tavern in the town. . . ."

"In the town," sang the boys.

"And there my true love sits him down. . . ."

"Sits him down. . . ."

He nearly raised the roof, quantity rather than quality. But it was terrific. Time after time he sang it. They wouldn't let him go and that bull-like voice roared on. It was so infectious I found myself joining in. At last, reluctantly, they let him go. And, as it was a drinking song, it's not surprising that the hall practically cleared to the nearest pub.

I sat there, hypnotised. He really did something for the boys and maybe for me too. Because when a small young soldier sat beside me, I didn't run away. He had a puffy face and didn't look more than sixteen.

"Would ye like to go fer a walk?" he asked in a Scottish accent.

I hestitated. I'd be disobeying my mother, but the boy was far from home. Could there be any harm in it? "Well, all right. But it'll have to be a short one. I have to go home."

And so I walked out for the first time. My young man was a bugler called Oswald. We walked together every night after that, usually along Queen's Parade. We'd find a seat there and sit huddled against the cold and make plans and dream dreams. He was going to be a great conductor and me a prima donna. Actually we talked of nothing but music. He never once put his arm around me or made any advance. Boys then would never fumble with your underwear. It was totally innocent and childish. After all we were only children.

But it couldn't last. Dad called for me one evening and I wasn't there. I didn't get into trouble, but there was a suspicion that I'd been deceitful.

"Bring Oswald home with you," Dad said. "There's no need to freeze to death along the sea front."

So reluctantly Oswald came home. He really was only a boy. I doubt if he'd begun to shave. But, lo and behold, he was practically a virtuoso on the piano. And all by ear. To me he was a genius and I sang like a true prima donna. Did he think I was great too? Probably. It was a case of mutual admiration.

My parents listened and gave him tea and sandwiches. But I never heard how he came to be a bugler. Or what happened to him.

One thing I knew — my dishwashing days were at an end.

20

Sunday was a day for visitors in our house. I suppose, it all started when Dad brought the hungry curates back from Evening Service to enjoy my mother's cooking. Our house became a sort of haven for them. Also, our pew was very popular with two or three local boys — there was no other room for them in all that large church. Then they walked us home, so it would have been discourteous not to ask them in. Mum always produced tea and sandwiches, buns and cake. Saturday was still her baking day. Everyone was turned out of the kitchen and the delicous smells tantalized us — soda bread, brown bread, buns, cakes, tarts and biscuits. The quantity depended on her mood.

At our repast goodies disappeared like snow off a ditch. You had to be pretty quick off the mark. Afterwards, there was music. At first, only hymns were allowed on Sundays, but by degrees other things crept in. Those curates fairly fancied themselves singing. I was no expert and had to fumble with the accompaniment. Probably it was a matter of luck if I hit the right note. But I don't think anyone noticed.

We sangs things like "Pale Hands I loved". "Excelsior" and "The Trumpeter" and many more nearly brought down the roof. Irish songs were not encouraged at the time, except "The Mountains of Mourne" and, of course, "Tipperary". There were other war songs. One began "A long, long trail a winding . . ." and another was "Roses of Picardy". We didn't know much about "Mademoiselle from Armentieres". But it was such fun and we all ended the evening washing dishes in the kitchen. Mum insisted.

The news from the front was bad. Place names like Ypres

and the Somme became too familiar to us. Hundreds were being killed every day. Bangor families kept hoping that the all too familiar telegram wouldn't be delivered to their door. But they hoped in vain. Every Evensong ended with the Rector reading the names of the latest victims from the chancel. When he finished the organ clashed out with great chords and shivers ran down one's back. "The Dead March in Saul" or "Flowers of the Forest" brought ready tears. Mr Jones, the organist, gave his best and was good. "He had to fortify himself for the weekly ordeal," people said. One Sunday evening the names of my Sunday School teacher's three brothers were read out, one after the other. The youngest was only eighteen. That was a terrible evening.

Then it was rumoured that the Ulster Division was practically wiped out. That Sunday evening, name after name was read out by the Rector. There wasn't a dry eye in the house. The dead truly marched in Saul that evening. It was a sad and tearful little party that trailed home to Mum, who still hardly ever went to church.

We found her in the drawing room waiting for us.

"Well, how many?" she asked.

"He read out a long list," I said, holding back tears.

Dad sighed heavily. "I'm afraid the Ulster Division's taken an awful battering."

Then the usual visitors began to arrive. The curates, of course, and a few stragglers, who came I'm sure for Mum's cooking.

But that evening she suddenly announced, "There's a change of menu tonight!"

Several faces perked up. Maybe it was a delicious dinner? Roast beef and gravy perhaps?

"Eh, what is it?" someone murmered politely.

"Porridge!" announced my mother, heading for the dining room.

Porridge? Unbelievingly, we trooped after her to view the impeccably laid table with its damask cloth and napkins and sparkling silver. It couldn't be true. Yet it was. At each place there was a soup plate of porridge.

We took our places in silence.

Dad said grace, "Bless us Lord and this food to our use for Christ's sake."

"Amen," we answered solemnly.

It was overdone. What was she thinking of? How could she shame us like this? But we supped manfully. Then, as Mum and Dad cleared the plates, someone began to giggle — probably Helen.

The Curate cleared his throat. "Delicious porridge, if I may say so, Mrs Breen."

"Thank you!" Mum disappeared into the kitchen and came back out with a plate of her sandwiches which she plonked down on the table. "There, you are! Have you room for more?"

Then Dad appeared with coffee.

At that, everyone was laughing.

Dad's vein was throbbing as if about to laugh too, but Mum was still deadly serious.

As we tucked in to the delicous feed, some brave soul dared to ask, "Why did we have to eat the porridge first, Mrs Breen?"

"It was penitential," she said solemnly.

We looked at each other. Penitential porridge? Who ever heard of such a thing?

"Our boys are dead," she said. "Thousands of them. I just can't bear to think of it. I had to make some gesture. All I could think of was porridge — which no one likes."

That was certainly true.

She got up and left the room.

Penitential porridge — that's how we mourned the Ulster Brigade. I hope God understood.

It was relief to return to the drawing room which was soon echoing with the old familiar tunes. As usual, I struck the occasional wrong note and, as usual, our musical Curates lead the choruses. But it wasn't the same. Before long on that sad

Sunday evening we were singing hymns and Mum was crying openly. We finished up with, "Oh, God our help in ages past".

Then Dad started the National Anthem, "God save our gracious King, God save our King."

Everyone joined in. I'll never forget the fervour of it.

As I went to sleep that night, the faraway Lambeg drums were beating out their own sad farewell. "See the sons of Ulster marching to the Somme," as a present day poet pithily put it. Critics today, are only too well aware of the stupidity and sheer waste of the whole operation. They'd probably go further and denouce the whole war and the way it was waged. The generals would come in for a severe trouncing. But that wouldn't bring back the dead — a whole generation of young men in their prime. I suppose it started the first cracks in the Empire. But that clock can't be turned back either. Those who were left muddled through. There was nothing else to do.

21

Most of the rest of the war is a sort of blur. Life went on, as it always does. We attended a secondary school in Bangor, run by qualified women. There's nothing much to say about it, except that it was boring. What schoolgirl likes school? They're all the same and all awful. I spent many hours singing in the Abbey Church choir. My sisters even joined it, but I suspect they were only interested in the social aspects of it. It was an excuse to get out from under the parental eye and my parents soon cottoned on to this and instructed them to resign. They weren't much loss, except pictorially. We were at that awkward age — past the little girl stage, but not yet young ladies. We were either "too young" or "too old" for everything, it seemed. As the oldest by fourteen months, I felt superior. But anytime I assumed my rightful authority, I was told where to get off by my sisters — accompanied by their ribald laughter. In some ways I was different from the other two, who occasionally ganged up on me. Nan was a go-getter and Helen full of life — perhaps she had some subconcious clue about her future.

On more than one occasion, I heard myself referred to by people outside the family as, "the plain one." This left me without any vanity but with an inward urge to "show them". But I kept this to myself. We had few rows and as a family were close knit. Tell-tales were taboo and we settled our differences between ourselves. We aided and sheltered each other on the whole. Especially in the matter of stockings.

Stockings were always either black or brown — no in between — and woollen in winter and lisle in summer. Unless we were going bare-legged.

I can see Mumper on winter evenings, sitting on one side of our dining room fire with a piled basket of stockings. And Dad on the other side — usually reading to us. He read Shakespeare's plays of all things, taking the different parts himself. And sometimes the Bible, the Song of Solomon was a favourite — I suppose that's where we all got a taste for poetry. Afterwards we went off to bed, shedding our clothes on the stairs all ready to drop off in the coldness of the upstairs rooms.

Stockings as we grew older were the bane of our lives, especially darned ones. We hated having to wear them. Then somebody put the notion into our heads that we could get new stockings on tick in S G Montgomery's. All we had to do was put it on our mother's account. A marvellous idea, which we acted on at once.

I wonder we weren't immediately caught out.

But a day of reckoning did, of course, arrive.

"What does this mean?" Mum asked, waving a bill.

I tried to look innocent. "Eh, what is it, Mumper?"

She pushed the bill in front of me. "Hose, hose, hose. Nothing but hose."

I felt myself redden. "We — eh — bought them."

She looked furious. "You what?"

"On your account."

"Well, hear me! I'm putting a notice in the paper that I won't be responsible for my daughters' debts."

We had a local paper — "The Spectator" and for a while this threat hung over us. But it did the trick. That's all there was about it. No fuss, nothing. It certainly was a very effective way of stopping that rot. Legs were not glamorous in those days. For the most part they were covered up by long, trailing skirts. So it didn't really matter what you wore, because nobody saw you.

Directly opposite our house there was what was called a "Posting Establishment." Naturally, there was a large arched gateway for the horses and vehicles to enter and emerge. But it also offered a good vantage point for the crowds of young soldiers who thronged the streets in the periods of time when they were released from their barracks in the surrounding areas. They all looked exactly the same in their badly cut, un-attractive khaki. Some had the knack of rolling on the obligatory puttees which were part of the uniform — coarse, black army boots didn't do anything to enhance the utilitarian outfit.

We three girls gave them the "once over" at intervals. From behind the lace curtains of the drawing room windows we had a good view and heated discussions as to which was the best or the worst of the bunch. We got a lot of fun out of it.

"I'll have that one," said Nan.

"No, he's mine!" I whispered. "You have the other one."

Helen, our baby, wasn't a strong contender. "That one's picking his nose. Yuk!"

Nan waved down at a boy who was smiling up. "Look at his puttees. He's got a cap that's too small for him."

"Hmm," I said. "Probably his head swelled since he joined the army."

"You're only saying that because I like him." Nan was always very certain about her likes and dislikes.

These boys were the latest that could be scraped up from England, Scotland, Wales. Country yokels, or the smarter townees, a motley crowd, all herded together and recruited to fill the great empty gaps left by the dead.

Their eyes were, of course, diverted from the street with its passers-by to our window. Inevitably, they began shouting back at us and whistling.

"Hey, georgeous!"

"'Allo, sweetheart!"

We had to do a disappearing act before being caught. Mum and Dad did catch us once and read the riot act loud and clear. But it did no good. It was a great game and I'm sure they knew full well what was going on. We got to know some of the faces which appeared regularly. But that was as far as it went.

We waved and smiled and blew kisses at our boy soldiers. But because of the class system we were quite unattainable and in an ivory tower. Finally they gave us up as a bad job and found girls in the town. They came and went and finally disappeared altogether.

One day a few officers appeared in the gateway. They were gorgeous creatures and, as usual, Nan and I picked out one each and waved.

But they gave no hint of having seen us. They were probably genuinely seeking shelter and uninterested in surveying the scene for cheap thrills or waving to young girls in windows.

We waved again, but they ignored us.

"Maybe they want a formal introduction," Nan said gloomily.

"I don't see how we can arrange that. We don't know anyone they know." I moved away from the window, feeling despondent.

Whether they saw us or not, we didn't know. Boys and young men were not in our line. Girls then were supposed to be modest creatures and it was up to the male of the species to make the first move.

But the two beautiful young officers appeared again and again. And more and more we wanted to talk to them. But things were at a deadlock.

One fateful afternoon, we saw them again in the gateway. They checked that we were there, as usual. Then, when we waved, they gave a gay salute and marched across the street.

The front door bell rang imperiously.

Nervously we had a fit of the giggles. No way were we going to answer that bell.

"Will someone answer the door!" Mum called out.

But wild horses wouldn't have moved us. We were anchored to our seats.

Then horror on horror, we heard Dad's firm footsteps going downstairs. We heard him open the door, then there was quite a conversation. Then footsteps on the stairs.

"They're coming upstairs!" Nan whispered.

Glory be to heaven, what were we to do now?

"Dad'll be so cross." Nan had gone pale.

I quaked inwardly. "I wish Mum were here!"

Then the door opened and there was Dad, grinning like a cheshire cat. Two hatless young men peered over his shoulders. They were taller than he was and he was a tall man.

"These young men say they'd like to know you," he said.

He sounded so funny we all burst out laughing. It looked as if he approved of them.

But we were speechless. Luckily he did the honours. "Let me introduce my daughters, Muriel and Anne — we call her Nan."

"Tony Hunt," one of the beautiful creatures said, his cap tucked under one arm as he extended a hand.

"Nelson Wright," said the other, doing the same.

We still couldn't speak.

"Won't you gentlemen sit down?" Dad said, filling in the gap. "I'll go and find your Mum."

There was a moment's silence.

"We're stationed at Holywood," Tony said, breaking the ice.

Then we all began talking together.

Tony was typically English, brownish and goodlooking. He hailed from somewhere near Bristol, while Nelson came from the North Country. They had met each other at Sandhurst after being in OTC at their schools. Then they were posted to the same regiment. Neither of them looked more than twenty.

"I'm just dead scared the whole thing'll be over before we can get a bash at the Germans," Tony said.

It was our first encounter with English boys. We had never been out of Ireland and thought their English accents the last word in sophistication and elegance. Soon, we were getting along nicely.

Then Mum and Dad reappeared on the scene.

"Will you stay to tea?" Mum enquired in the usual Irish way.

Tony looked quickly at Nelson, saying, "Eh — I think we ought to be getting along."

Nelson cleared his throat awkwardly. "Yes — we should be getting back."

They didn't know what to do. Perhaps a cup of tea would commit them to something when they were just giving us the once over.

"Sit down there, you'll have a cup of tea!" Dad said, as Mum, undaunted, disappeared down the stairs in the direction of the kitchen.

In a very few minutes she produced a marvellous tea: homemade scones, sandwiches and cake. And did they do justice to it? I'd never seen such appetites in my life. Did the army not feed them?

"It's just like home," Tony said, standing up. "I'm afraid we'll have to rush now."

"Yes, we have to catch a train back to Holywood." Nelson always echoed him.

Tony gave me a ravishing smile. He looked tentatively at Dad, "Can we come back next week?"

"Certainly! We'd love to see you," Dad said affably.

Nelson looked hungrily at the empty plates. "Eh, can we bring our friends?"

Mum was a bit taken aback. She glanced at Dad who was looking away. "Certainly! Come back as soon as you like and we'd be delighted to see your friends."

They clattered down the stairs and, with a gay farewell, took themselves off.

"Goodness knows what we've let ourselves open to," Mum said worriedly. "Those boys would eat you out of house and home."

Dad started to clear the dishes. "They're growing lads, Liz."

She sighed. "Never mind, things could be worse. We'll manage."

Mum could always manage. Obviously she was now thinking of our rations and how difficult it was to make ends meet. Actually, we got plenty of parcels from our friends in the country, as there was no rationing there. I don't remember that we wanted for anything. But Mum liked to think it was just as bad for us as it was for the British.

It was only a few days before they arrived again. There was a third one with them who had obviously only come for the "eats." He wasn't interested in us and we ignored him. Tony, inasmuch as he could, appropriated me and the other boy fell for Nan. But we were very much under the watchful eye of our Mum who didn't give us much time to improve the acquaintance. But there was nothing we could do about it. Boyfriends were unheard of in our house. We were quite inexperienced — it was a disadvantage not to have brothers. So we could only wait and see what these strange English boys would do. If anything.

Imagine our surprise when one day they arrived in a motor car. A two seater. Cars were only just beginning to be seen on the streets and were owned by only a few people. Charabancs, as they were called then, were also beginning to appear. Our whole family went down to the street to see it.

I looked at it with awe. "How can you possibly afford it, Tony?"

"It's a joint venture. We bought it between us. And it's not exactly new."

"It looks new," Dad inspected the wheels.

"Ah, no, sir!"

"What's that for?" Dad pointed to a stick.

"The brake, sir."

We stared in the windows, while its various points were explained to us. By this time a crowd had gathered round it. It was a curiosity in Bangor, but the boys were uneasy at the attention they were drawing. They were afraid that something would happen to the car.

"Can we take Muriel and Nan for a little ride, sir," Tony asked.

Dad looked at Mum.

"You'll be careful of them?" she said anxiously.

"On my honour, they'll be as safe as houses."

Dad nodded, saying firmly. "Well, have them back in time for tea."

"You'll have to wear coats and tie something round your heads," Tony said. "You've no idea how breezy it is."

So with due preparation and much advice from Mum and Dad, we approached the vehicle. The crowds stood back and allowed us to ascend. Tony was driving and after many puffings and blowings and false starts, we finally moved off amidst a rousing cheer. We gathered speed going down the main street and people stood to stare.

The car was quite high and open to every breeze.

"We'll go to Groomsport!" Tony shouted.

Nelson navigated. "Take the shore road!"

We passed through Ballyholme at an average speed of about twenty-five miles an hour. We hooted and tooted at every street corner and reduced speed to walking rate at the corners. With our scarves flying and horn tooting we made almost a royal appearance.

We were thrilled and maybe a little scared as well — our very first drive in a real motor car. We finally reached Groomsport and it was decided we'd have a drink.

"What'll you have?" Tony gallantly asked. "We're having a beer."

"I'll have beer too," Nan said.

"No, she'll have lemonade. We'll both have lemonade!" I said.

"But I've never had beer," she hissed malevolently.

I ignored her, hoping the boys wouldn't get drunk. Strong drink was an abomination in our almost teetotal household. As a treat we got a mouthful of sherry at Christmas and on special occasions.

Nelson drove on the journey back and I sat on Tony's knee. He put his arms around me to keep me warm, he said. And Nan, who was only a little thing, squeezed in between the two boys. We made better speed now and I hoped it wasn't the beer. I wouldn't admit that the other boy might be a better driver.

Mum was looking anxiously out the window as we came chugging up the street.

When we pulled up she was at the front door to greet us with hugs and kisses. "Darlings, I was so worried."

You'd think we'd been to the North Pole.

"Praise be, you're all right."

It was embarassing.

"Will you come for a little spin?" Tony asked.

"I certainly won't!"

"Just up the street and back?" Nelsen coaxed.

But nothing would persaude her to put a foot in the thing.

After that it became a regular thing to snatch us from under the parental eye and hie us off for a drive. I suppose our parents thought it wouldn't last long. Sooner or later the boys would be sent "overseas," as it was euphemistically called. Their one dread was that the war might be over before they could fight.

22

The dreaded day of departure came. As it was the last time, we were given reluctant permission to dine with them in Donaghadee, of all places — it was a seaside town nearby and there was a nice hotel there. We had never dined in a hotel in all our young lives, so we were very excited. We got dolled up in our nicest frocks and, with many instructions and warnings from Mum, set off.

But it was a silent journey to Donaghadee. Our hearts were sad and the boys were not in their usual talkative mood. They had booked a table at the hotel and went straight into the dining room. After a little bit of titivating and tidying our hair, we followed them.

We were ushered to our lavishly decorated table by the head waiter. We were the only people in the room. The boys had decided an early meal would leave time to do something afterwards.

All went well. I chose from the menu and so did Nan.

Then the wine waiter came. "What will you have to drink, sir?"

Tony glanced casually at the wine list. "Oh, I think, a house red for us and lemonade for the ladies."

"Claret would be nice," Nan said firmly.

I looked at my younger sister. Claret? What on earth was Claret?

The boys looked at each other and grinned. The wine waiter put his hand over his mouth and soon everybody was giggling.

"We've got quite a good claret, sir," he said eventually.

So claret it was — only a red wine and not even fizzy. I

didn't like it, but Nan drank her glassful and the boys finished the bottle. It was a hilarious meal, but we got through it and were served coffee in style in another room.

It was still very early.

"What'll we do now?" I asked. It was too soon to go home and, perish the thought, we might never see the boys again.

Tony had made up his mind. "I'm going to row you to the Copelands."

"But — they're miles and miles away. It'll take hours."

"Nevertheless, that's where we're going." And, nodding at Nelson and Nan, he took me firmly by the arm and walked quickly up the pier where a rowing boat was waiting.

It must've been arranged, as the others drove off. But it was a glorious summer evening and the sea was as calm as a mill pond. I was quickly propelled down the steps into the boat.

Off came Tony's cap and jacket and he took up the oars which he handled in a workman-like way. There were no words to describe the loveliness of the evening. So I sat still, admiring Tony's rowing. He was no novice and that was certain. The Copelands, which seemed so far, were suddenly very near. He coasted round a bit, until he found a suitable place to land. Then he secured the boat and, lifting me in his arms, deposited me on a lovely grassy bank. Not a soul was in sight, only a few sheep in the distance. And the birds flying over us.

I lay back and closed my eyes.

Then Tony kissed me. He kissed me over and over again.

"I love you," he said, as if he'd just discovered something important. "I really love you."

And so we lay there content to be in each other's arms. At least I was content. It might've been different for Tony. In those days girls were virgins until they were married. Tony knew there was nothing more to be expected. I didn't even know where babies came from or how one went about getting them. But I was loved and that was almost the same as being proposed to. I'm sure that's how Tony meant it. It was the most thrilling, exciting day in my life. What heaven to be loved.

"I'm so happy," I whispered, staring at the segulls.

"Me too."

But it was soon time to go. I stumbled back onto the boat, drugged with happiness. My own beautiful Tony. Mine, for ever and ever, Amen. And he felt the same.

I can't remember where Nelson and Nan went but they were waiting by the pier and we drove home together. There were tearful farewells and a curious Mum who did not ask one solitary question. Nor did my Dad.

And so off they went to the awful, bloody Front. The war seemed to be getting more vicious in its final stages. Nan's boy was killed by a stray bullet soon after they landed. It was a freak accident, but somehow typical of all that stupid waste. I had to endure months of anxiety about Tony. I heard nothing. Then, suddenly, the war was over.

Little Bangor was the same as everywhere else. People went wild with excitement. They didn't know whether to laugh or cry. The lights went up and the bands played. We were on streets with everyone else, dancing and kissing total strangers.

But when would my Tony come. Or would he ever? Would they send him back to England, or post him to some foreign land? Strangely, they did none of those things. They sent him back to Ireland to his old barracks, but he knew it was only temporary.

The War had changed him. Also the loss of his friend. So it was a much quieter Tony who presented himself in due course at our house. It was a joyful reunion, of course, and my family treated him like a hero. And it worked.

We were tactfully left to our own devices. After all, I was nearly eighteen now.

"Nice Tony," my father called him, almost the same way as he'd have said, "Nice dog."

But one day Tony said, "I've bought a small sailing boat, Muriel."

Oh, dear. I wasn't altogether jumping with joy. Sailing boats weren't my favourite thing. One was supposed to do all sorts of things one didn't like — cold, wet, scary things. Unlike Nan, who took such things in her stride, I was no sea-dog.

But Tony adored it and would regularly sail down to Bangor or Donaghadee, single-handed. He preferred Donaghadee and willy-nilly I had to go there to meet him. Luckily, I had friends living there who made me welcome. But all this came to an end.

One cold, wet, stormy evening with huge seas running, Tony announced he was sailing back to Holywood.

"Haven't you heard the coastguard's warnings?" I argued.

"Ah, I don't need to worry about them."

And off he went. The coastguards at Orlock look-out reported that he was making progress against the odds. But they spoke too soon. He was shipwrecked off Groomsport and only just made it, swimming to the shore. Fishermen pulled him out of the sea, saying the boat would be salvaged. And someone gave him dry clothes and someone else, who luckily owned a car, offered to drive him back to the barracks in time.

Time is of the essence in a soldier's life and it was remorselessly closing in on that brief interlude of innocent romance. The day came when he told me he was going to Egypt with his regiment. There were fond farewells and promises of eternal devotion, which we both sincerely meant. Then off he went to bid farewell to his English family.

Then to my surprise, a letter came from his mother to my mother.

"They want you to meet them in London," she said. "They're staying at the Langham Hotel for a few days to do some shopping."

My heart missed a beat.

But she shook her head and Dad looked grave.

There was much thought given to that letter and I think

now the right decision was taken. The answer was no. I was too young, too inexperienced. I'd never been in England and I couldn't travel alone. There were a thousand and one reasons and all of them legitimate.

It was probably a relief to Tony's mother. A boy, a girl, and a romance that would not last. And what did she know about a little Irish girl?

And so he went off to faraway Egypt. Letters and snapshots of Tony doing this, that and the other began to arrive. We wrote to each other every single day. He sent me little bits of Egyptian jewellery, but, of course, it couldn't last. One day he wrote, saying that his CO had told him he was not behaving in a gentlemanly manner. That he was keeping me on a string so to speak.

That's how it ended. I was not heartbroken. There were always plenty of boys hanging about and they were on the spot. A few years later one more letter arrived. He told me he was going to marry his CO's daughter. But by that time I was engaged.

Years and years later, a funny thing happened. I was living in London and waiting my turn at the dentist's. Idly I turned over the old magazines that seem to be the feature of every waiting room. I picked up an old *Tatler* and there, before my astonished eyes, was Tony. He stood in the middle of a large group and the caption mentioned that he was the Colonel of the Regiment. I was tempted to write but didn't. I thought about "The Colonel's lady and Judy O'Grady" being sisters under the skin. Did he ever give a thought in all those years to the little Irish girl he left behind? I drank his health that night, just for luck.

23

The First World War changed everything. More than anything, it brought about the liberation of women. They had to take men's places in factories, so up went the skirts and off went the hair. The suffragettes had fought for the vote and this was now granted. Although, I have to admit, that movement passed me by. It just didn't get to Bangor and anyway my father thought it silly. Besides, I was far too frivolous to take any notice of it. I was only interested in having fun.

The age of flapperdom had arrived and with it came even more freedoms. The whole world seemed to be dancing — the Dansant, Foxtrots, One Steps, and the Charleston. Girls wore short skirts and carried long cigarette holders. Gaiety was not only at "Phil the Fluter's Ball", youth was breaking out all over. The post war generation was "rarin" to go" and we were carried along with it willy nilly. Idiotic songs were on everyone's lips:

> Let's all sing like the birdies sing,
> Tra, la-la, la.

There was outraged shock when I had my long brown hair cut off.

My father gaped. "But where are your lovely long plaits?"

The main problem for Joe and Liz was that their daughters were growing up. Although I had just left school, they hadn't any concrete plans for launching me — or any of us — on an academic career. Money wasn't plentiful and, in those days, girls didn't usually go to the university. There were only a few careers open to women: teaching, medicine, or secretarial work. You could also be a companion. It had to be something ladylike, a concept that held no interest for me. A few girls went to Queens University, but they wanted to be teachers or doctors, which I didn't. So, my parents wisely decided I wasn't university material. They probably thought optimistically, "Oh, she'll get married and live happily ever after." And they were quite entitled to think along those lines. The house was always full of boys and young men.

In the meantime, a banking career was decided on. Banks were then opening up to female employees for the first time, due to a shortage of manpower caused by the war. So, at the age of eighteen-plus and in fear and trepidation, I was summoned to appear before a Board at the Ulster Bank in Belfast.

I was scared stiff. The interview was a nightmare to me, also the test. But, apparently, I acquitted myself well. At any rate I was notified that I'd passed the test and told to present myself on a certain date at their Head Office in Belfast.

All commuters to Belfast seemed to travel on the eight-twenty, so it was decided I would too. The only stricture was that I had to travel first class. There could be no mixing with the plebs in second class — the more popular one for my age group apparently. The fateful morning arrived and I was seen off by the whole family.

I'll swear my mother was crying. "Have you got your ticket somewhere safe?"

Dad looked worried. "Take care coming out of the station."

Although the bank was considered a good career for girls, we were a rarity and kept very much in the background. Especially in the Head Office where I was working. But I loved it. I was a new woman, one of the first to work for a living. I'm sure it was very menial work, and the hours were long, but I got real money for it and Saturdays were free. I assumed a new status in my own estimation. It's probably just as well I had two sisters to remind me that I was only a very small cog in the big Ulster Bank. I think they were jealous actually, as they were still incarcerated in the school for Young Ladies. Sometimes when I looked at them dispassionately, I had to admit I had two very pretty sisters, one fair, the other dark.

I don't know where I met Alexander MacMonagle Segerdal. He was a young doctor, qualified for three or four years and six or seven years older than me. He was handsome, in a way, with reddish hair and specs, and his trousers were always at half-mast. But although he pursued me relentlessly, the attraction was not mutual.

I couldn't get rid of him. Eventually, he ended up in our house where he was awarded the "not bad" rating. Even my father tolerated him. Of course, my mother twigged from the first that his intentions were honourable. I was already a "wife to be." Number One daughter had made it. And all mothers then wanted their daughters settled. Marriage was a career for girls.

But Number One daughter was not so sure. Actually "Sugar," as we all called him, fell a long way short of my ideal husband material. The only thing in his favour was his difference — he was half Swedish.

His mother, a tiny Belfast girl, had met and married a large fair haired Swede who was in the Diplomatic Service of his country and based in China. They had three sons in quick succession who, in due course, were sent as boarders to Campbell College. Their maternal grandfather was editor of a strongly Presbyterian paper in Belfast and their grandmother kept a beady eye on their welfare.

It can't have been a satisfactory arrangement because the three of them were finally installed in a house in the Botanic Avenue area with a suitable housekeeper. I suppose they joined their parents in China at stated periods. It was not a normal upbringing and my mother took Sugar under her wing, deciding he needed mothering. Dad got to like him too and my sisters took great glee in laughing at him. But it was plain I was the light of his eyes.

Still, I got a shock and surprise when he asked me to marry him. We were sitting on the rocks at Pickie, our feet blissfully dabbling in a warm little pool.

"Eh — would you do me the honour of being my wife, Muriel?" He looked at me through his specs, his reddish face redder from the sun.

My heart jumped in dismay. "What?"

He took my hand. "I'd be greatly honoured if you'd consent to being my wife. You realise that although not profitably employed at the moment, I have a good future and will be able to provide you with every possible comfort. In time, that is."

I laughed. He looked so serious. But it was a serious matter, I suppose, and I half-heartedly agreed.

So home we went and Sugar, to my surprise, clinched the matter formally by asking my father permission to marry his daughter.

Poor Dad gave it, and was visibly touched. He put his hand on me. "This is my greatest treasure."

I was very embarrassed. I felt so unworthy.

"You take care of her," he added.

My mother made no bones about the matter. She was delighted. "Now I have a son."

"Eh — thank you, Mrs Breen."

Perhaps she'd always wanted a son? I should have been happy. I had reached the goal of a girl's life — marriage. But it stuck in my gullet. Why did one have to get married? Life at the bank was fun. Would Sugar be fun? He was inclined to be dull, and his half-mast trousers were eccentric. There were other things which put me off him. Things which all came together in an odd way. While looking for a suitable position, he had taken a post in the Belfast Lunatic Asylum at Purdysburn — they were called that then which was horrible. Although he had his own delightful quarters there, it was a huge place that terrified me — I felt so sorry for the inmates. I think I was depressed and frightened at the thought of what could happen to a human being. Mental illness was far more terrifying then. People were locked up and that was the end of them. Sugar certainly didn't want to be an ordinary GP — although that's how he ended up. He was interested in studying psychiatry, then in its infancy. But the atmosphere of the place depressed me so much I even began to think wickedly, that Sugar had an affinity with his charges.

But still it was fun being engaged. He bought me a conventional ring of five small diamonds, which gave me great pleasure. It was a nice ring and suitable, and I was getting used to him. I was still a virgin, of course, and would remain one till marriage. That was understood. But my ignorance was abysmal. "Any slut can have a baby in a ditch," was one of my shy mother's dire warnings to us girls. But that's all she ever said about the matter. I never knew where babies came from. Or how one had one.

Then Sugar's parents came home on leave and I was up for inspection. I must have passed, although there were the odd suggestions about hairstyle and clothes. But my heart really did fail me when his mother decided that my wedding dress would be made of chinese brocade. My wedding dress? I had put the subject on the long finger. Now they were talking about a dress. And then I'd be with Sugar for ever and ever.

The climax came when I was waiting in his study one day. Idly I cast my eyes on his bookcase and picked out a book at random. It was all about childbirth, illustrations and everything. It was my first real knowledge of where babies came from and an absolute shock. I was nearly sick. I swore that nobody, nobody was ever going to do that to me. I'd never, ever get married.

A week later I gave Sugar back his ring. And nothing in heaven or on earth would make me change my mind.

I'll draw a decent veil over the consequent events. My mother was furious, absolutely furious.

"Are you crazy?" she raged.

But I was obdurate. "I can't marry him."

"No man would ever look at a girl who could do such a dreadful thing."

Sugar was devastated — especially when I wouldn't even consent to see him again. And I was in the doghouse at home.

My father said nothing. He seemed to understand, but he looked weary. Was it imagination that he'd lost weight? He was slimmer than ever and his collars were too big.

I know I treated Sugar very badly, but have never regretted not marrying him. Looking down the years I try to persuade myself I did him a favour. But the medical books were what clinched it. Girls then were told nothing. It's so much better now when things are talked about more. It's not so frightening.

24

But I missed Sugar's company and unfailing cheerfulness. Girls still never went anywhere unescorted and often I was left twiddling my thumbs when my sisters were out enjoying themselves. But I was never tempted to change my mind — well, hardly ever. If I did, it would be impossible. Marriage meant being bound to Sugar for ever and ever and ever, and being expected to produce babies in that ghastly way. So, despite loneliness, isolation and disgrace, I stuck it out.

Then an unexpected diversion broke the tedium. One morning I was summoned to the secretary's office in the bank.

He coughed dryly. "We're quite pleased with your performance of your duties, Miss Breen."

I felt myself blush.

"I've called you in here to inform you that you're to report to our Clones branch."

Goodness, but where was Clones? "How long will I be there?"

"Just a few weeks. A girl is ill. The manager insists on having someone to replace her."

And that was that. I wasn't given any choice in the matter. I was informed, not asked. The secretary went on to inform me about the cost of a railway ticket and lodgings, etc.

"You live in Bangor, don't you?" he asked.

"In that case, you'd better go home and and pack for a stay of a few weeks."

My first thought, of course, was would Dad and Mum allow me to go? I had never spent a night away from home alone before. But now I was a working woman and would have to do what the Bank ordered.

Disappointingly, the news was taken quite calmly by my parents. Maybe they gave me credit for having some sense. Or else they were adept at hiding their doubts.

Anyway I arrived in Clones without difficulty and made my way to the Bank. It wasn't hard to find. Clones to my eyes was just a dull Irish country town. The Diamond was the principal feature and all the important buildings were there — banks, churches, some shops, post office and some ancient-looking Solicitor's offices. All in all, my first impressions were of dullness. And to add to the dreariness, a fine Irish mist enveloped everything.

With a sinking heart, I found my destination. Actually, I was rather surprised, because the inside was brightly lit and a few customers were being served. A young man behind the counter looked pretty normal. He must've twigged who I was, because I was shown into the Manager's Office.

He was a nice friendly middle-aged man who looked at me with some surprise. "Ah, Miss Breen, you're the eh — replacement for eh — Miss McOliver."

I nodded awkwardly.

He stared at me. "You're rather young. You've — eh — only recently joined the Bank?"

"Yes."

"I'm sure you'll like Clones. We've arranged for you to stay in Miss McOliver's digs. She finds them satisfactory."

"Will I be here for long?"

He shook his head. "Miss McOliver's a strong country girl. She should be able to resume work in a few weeks. You must be tired now. I'll ask a junior to take you to the house."

The junior was in my age bracket, but at the acne stage. At first he was painfully shy and didn't seem able to give me a bird's eye picture of the general scene. But when his tongue loosened, it wagged merrily. But the prognosis wasn't very promising.

The detached house which was our destination looked all right from the outside.

"The family's all boys," said junior. "Father's deceased, so the mother takes in lodgers." Then he quickly deserted me at the gate.

An untidy middle-aged woman opened the door in response to my knock. "Come in. You'll be the new girl. I was told you'd probably come today. I've put clean sheets on Mary's bed. Her things are still there, but there'll be plenty of room for your clothes."

"I'm sure that will be fine," I said, following her inside.

She looked disparagingly at my small suitcase.

I clutched it firmly. "Eh — I won't be here for long."

When we reached the bedroom, I looked about in dismay. It was something new in the line of bedrooms. It looked for all the world like a converted passageway. There were two doors, "in" and "out," so to speak.

"Don't worry, you won't be disturbed," the landlady said, before I could comment.

"Oh." I stared at the bleak little room.

"We all go to bed very early."

Goodness, I thought, it really is a passageway. But I said nothing. "Wait and see." is sometimes a good policy. Besides it mightn't be as bad as it seemed.

"You'll be wanting your tea," my landlady said grudgingly.

"What time do you serve meals?" I enquired politely.

"I've no fixed time. It's usually a fry and that doesn't take long."

My heart sank further into my shoes. What sort of place had I come to?

The next twenty-four hours were an eye opener to me. All meals were served in the kitchen on a corner of the table, just beside the range. I never got anything but a fry, a greasy one at that. And all night people were passing through my bedroom, as if it were a public highway.

After two days I decided I was leaving — even if I had to resign from the Bank. And on the third morning, I packed my things and said goodbye.

The landlady looked up from the range. Then glanced curiously down at my case. "Goodbye?"

"Yes." I summoned all my courage. "And I won't be back."

The woman looked at me in amazement. I could almost read her thoughts and they weren't complimentary to me.

I hadn't said anything to the bank, so it was a big surprise when I arrived with my bag. I must've looked a sorry sight, for I was immediately despatched upstairs to the manager's wife.

She soon sorted me out.

"We've a spare room here," she said. "You'd better stay, until we find something more suitable."

She had three sons and no daughters and was well used to dealing with emergencies. I couldn't believe my luck. Even if it was only for a night or two, there had to be decent digs somewhere. But apparently there weren't, and I settled in as if I were one of the family. They were musical and great fun and I was in the right age group.

Today, Clones is a border town, part in Northern Ireland and part in the South. The war against Britain was being fought in the early twenties, so it was a dangerous place to live. It was the first place I heard talk of terrorists, now known as the IRA. Although I didn't really see anything, there was an atmosphere of unease. So, despite the extreme kindness of that charming family, I was not sorry to leave.

I'd only been back in the fold a few weeks, when I was despatched to Lurgan. This was completely different. There was no choice about digs — you were automatically booked into the YWCA.

It was clean and bare with basic food. There were three or four girls to a bedroom. Most were from the country and worked in shops in the town. There was a pecking order among working women at the time — a teacher was considered higher than a secretary and a shop girl higher than a servant. As a bank employee, I was considered a bit special and given preferential treatment. This mainly meant sitting beside the superintendant at breakfast. The fare was normally porridge, bread and butter and marmalade — no eggs. Imagine my surprise when I was offered the top of the superintendant's egg as a further treat?

"I, eh — don't like eggs," I stammered.

Frugality and cleanliness were the passwords of the establishment. But it was value for money and that was probably why it was always full. Work was dull and I was glad when my time there came to an end and I returned to work in Belfast. My family welcomed me home with open arms. I was now much more important in their eyes.

The Bank must've thought I could fit in anywhere, because I was soon told that I'd been appointed permanently to Donaghadee. What a surprise! Donaghadee was not much more than a fishing village then and about as inaccessible as the moon from Bangor. My family could see no solution but digs again.

I got to Donaghadee in some sort of hired vehicle. The war was over but everything was still in short supply. There were two routes: the scenic, seaside one through Groomsport; and the shorter, inland one with only fields to look at — which I was to know very well.

The Bank was in a side street. It was a smallish house, converted, with two ordinary windows — barred, of course — and a formidable door with the Ulster Bank proclaimed importantly over it. At a tight squeeze, there might have been room for half a dozen customers. There was a thick glass wall at one end with a door marked Manager's Office. In this sanctum, he interviewed customers. Otherwise he sat in the middle of the counter in front of the door leading to his apartment — the rest of the house. The counter took up a good deal of space. The cashier presided at one end and at the other end was a high Victorian-style stool and a sort of desk with a glass panel to shield me from the eyes of the curious.

Mr Ringland, the manager, was tall with a paunch, a bald head and a drooping walrus-like moustache. He was a bachelor and seemed old to me.

"We've found digs for you, Miss Breen," he said when I arrived. "Over a small knick-knack shop further up the street."

"They're only temporary, I'm afraid. They're booked up for the summer months," added the cashier. He was also small with a drooping moustache and a luxuriant head of iron grey hair. He had the incredible name of Servitus Theodore Smith.

They both looked at me doubtfully. I'm sure the last thing they wanted in the place was a gay female, young enough to be their daughter.

My new landlady, Mrs McClure, was pregnant. She too eyed me up and down as if I were some strange specimen. There was no pretence of welcome.

"You'll have the room above the shop to sit in," she snapped. And the back bedroom."

A least it was spic and span.

I reported for duty the next morning and was admitted at the front door by the housekeeper. She was a little grey woman with a twinkle in her eye. "The manager will be right down."

Then Mr Ringland appeared in bedroom slippers, with a clinking of the keys attached to his person. He opened the inner door and I started work. No sign of Mr Smith. I learned before long that he was always late.

There weren't many customers that first day. The few who came in gaped at me. A girl, a young girl in a bank. Who ever heard of such a thing? I was responsible for the ledgers and the customers' pass books. Also, I was entrusted with the stamp book and was responsible for all outgoing mail. The manager, of course, opened all incoming post.

We were an incongruous trio, but I must say they were very nice to me, in an avuncular sort of way. I became intimate with Mrs Thompson, the housekeeper, who was probably glad of female company. Actually, the bank became a home from home.

There wasn't much to do in a small Irish seaside town. Bridge evenings and little dinner parties kept Mr Ringland from stagnation. In those days a bank manager was a bank manager. It meant something in a small town, and a bachelor was especially welcome. So he had a pleasant life, fishing at weekends and playing golf.

Mr Smith was altogether different. Although he was married and lived in a three storied house on the unfashionable side of town, he brought his lunch in a brown paper bag. Before long I was invited to go home with him and meet his wife. She was a beautiful, tiny, fragile creature — like something taken straight from a cameo. And was treated accordingly. He had a son, Charlie, at boarding school who was looked on as a sort of miracle. No one knew how they produced him. Mrs Smith was regarded as a saint. She never did a thing in the house, not even cooking. They had a daily maid of sorts to clean. Otherwise, Servitus Theodore was chief cook and bottle washer.

He was also an inventor. He had something that operated from their bedroom which lit the kitchen fire in the morning so that the kettle was boiling when he came downstairs. It didn't often work and that was why he was always late. He had gadgets for everything. I never knew what was in the navy blue cloth bag, closed with a drawstring, which he brought into his office every day — as well as his lunch. But I'm sure it was some new invention to do in slack moments. He was always fiddling with something. An unwordly, charming eccentric was Servitus Theodore.

One day he arrived late, as usual, and took off his hat with a flourish to reveal a full head of snow white hair. "Good morning, Muriel."

I tried not to stare. "Good morning, Servitus."

He looked like a portrait of Lloyd George. Was his grey hair a wig? Why had no one told me?

He touched his white thatch. "What do you think?"

"It's lovely."

"I thought I looked too youthful," he said apologetically. "This is more suitable for my age."

But it was a long time before I got used to his altered appearance. It changed him completely, both physically and mentally. He became an old man over night. I don't know what the customers thought, but I caught some sly grins.

But Servitus Theodore was a nice man, wig and all. There aren't many people like him nowadays. To the day he died he wrote me a long, long letter every Christmas in his funny crabbed handwriting. I loved getting them.

I soon knew all the inhabitants of Donaghadee. It was a dreary place in winter and I moved from one set of digs to another, all equally unsatisfactory. But a few people were kind to me. Finally, the Rector and his wife put me up. But they lived in a house large enough to house a battallion with the minimum of mod cons and an enormous garden.

But I was bored and, my family thought, half starved. Then someone came up with the idea of a motor bicycle. Although nobody had ever seen or heard of a girl on a motor bicycle, the idea had its merits. I could be in Donaghadee in less than half an hour and home in time for tea.

A New Imperial soon appeared in our backyard. But, although motor bicycles then were not the monsters of today, it terrified me. I could hardly ride an ordinary bike.

It took a lot of patient coaching before I had the nerve to venture out onto the public highway — escorted, of course. In time I became proficient, after a fashion. My sisters thought me an old fuddy-duddy, afraid of my own shadow. They would laugh riotously when I appeared dressed in an ensemble of waterproof trousers and jacket, a peaked cap and gauntlet gloves. There were no helmets worn in those days, more's the pity.

The day arrived when I was pronounced fit to undertake the journey to Donaghadee unaccompanied. So off I went, not knowing whether I was fit to cope with the vagaries of my steed. But all went well and I didn't exceed the speed limit.

With a sigh of relief, I arrived at the Post Office where the monster had to be housed till going-home time.

I began to be a source of local interest. People watched out to wave and laugh at me. Let's face it, there wasn't much else to look at. But a girl on a motor bicycle was a phenomenon. Still, I was never tempted to do more than go to Donaghadee and back. I had no desire to tour the country.

Then one day I hit the cow. It meandered out of a field, right in front of me. There was no time to swerve. It got it right in the midriff. The cow wasn't much the worse for the experience, and neither was I. But I developed a bad case of nerves. I seemed to loose my confidence or something. Then sometime later I had my bad accident. All I remember was a man coming out from behind one of those high backed carts. I swerved to avoid him and hit the pavement.

I awakened in the spare bedroom where a nurse was sitting at the window. My head, I discovered, was encased in ice bags and I felt very far away from everything — except the pain in my head. Apparently, I had been quickly picked up in Donaghadee and taken at once to the doctor's house as there was no hospital. I couldn't have been very bad, because I was nursed at home. But I had done something to the base of my skull, which left me deaf in one ear and prone to headaches.

Still, I was alive, and only by the grace of God, my anxious parents told me a hundred times. And it was a long time before I was announced fit to resume the hurly burly of life. I was treated as an invalid until my sisters intervened and said they were fed up with the attention I was getting. The New Imperial disappeared to my relief. Never again would I ride on a motor bicycle.

Finally, I reported back to Head Office in Belfast. There I became a sort of curiosity and, although I didn't know it, came under the special scrutiny of a young man called Frank. He was one of the up and coming young bankers who learnt about real banking behind the scenes. No counter work for them.

He was a canny young man, as befits a good banker. Imagine my surprise when he took rooms in a select part of Bangor. We travelled on the same train and eventually in the same carriage. I could feel his eye on me.

He was a good deal older, so I was flattered when he asked me out. "Like to go to the pictures one evening?"

Having nothing better to do, I agreed to meet him.

"Ask him in for coffee," mother said.

I wasn't sure whether I would or not — it depended. But I did — he had behaved royally to me. The best seats and a decent box of chocolates.

So he got the once-over from my parents and sisters. I could see he was nervous, but didn't know why.

"Call any time, Frank," my mother said, pouring the tea. "We are always pleased to see friends of the girls."

As she didn't say that to everybody, Frank had struck oil.

I wasn't so sure about my father. He didn't say much, and again I was aware that all was not well with him physically.

Some weeks later he called me aside.

"Don't play fast and loose with that fellow, Muriel."

"I'm not."

"If you're not serious, get rid of him."

I was annoyed. "I don't know what you mean."

"He's serious and I don't think you are."

Really it was none of his business. I could manage my own affairs and it was nice to receive presents. To only express a wish and have it fulfilled. If the idea of marriage crept into my head, I dismissed it quickly. Why did everyone have to get married? I had no intention of ever marrying anyone. After all, Frank was years older than me. He couldn't be serious.

Still, I remembered what my father said.

25

But talk of marriage took second place to the terrible news that my beloved father was very ill. He had something wrong with his sinus. I suppose it was cancer, I've never really known. I suppose I've never wanted to know. But they took him off to a special hospital in Belfast for treatment.

He was never what you'd call a big strong man, but slight. Now he seemed to fade away. My mother wouldn't go near him, except under protest. She could not physically watch him going further and further away from her. So I substituted. I couldn't see him enough. I spent hours with him.

But she was there when he died, fully *compos mentis*, and I was not.

They brought him home in a box. It stood on trestles in our dining room for a couple of days and I stayed with him. The coffin was never opened, so in our imagination he still lived. Only we couldn't see him. But it was a terrible time. "The birds of the air were a-sighing and a-sobbing," in my imagination.

They took him away eventually. In those days, women remained behind closed doors. They did not go to the cemetery, which was only for men. The ladies of the house usually prepared the funeral meats or whatever was offered to the returning mourners. In this case, I don't remember what happened. I don't even remember if we cooked, or anything at all about the next few days. We were all moving like ghosts in a denuded house.

Why did I love him so much? Why does any girl love her father? I was never my mother's favourite child, yet always number one with my father. Now he was gone. I thought about my early childhood when he looked after me. Of all those walks with him and our long, serious conversations. "There's no use in walking up a road with your eyes straight ahead," he would constantly say. "Look to the left and right. Be observant and you never know what you'll find." I remembered these sayings, his great inner goodness and wonderful sense of humour. He was completely unbiased politically. In all my life I never heard him run anyone down. He would've made a good clergyman, but instead he married and had us. And now we were alone.

My mother was ready to die too. She moved silently through the house, a small figure bundled up in my father's grey dressing gown. Finally, she took to her bed completely.

Strangely, Frank took over. He finally talked my mother into sanity. Although he bullied her a bit, he couldn't reach me. I resented him in a way. What business had he to be there, he wasn't a member of the family. Yet what would we do without him?

Gradually, we began to pick ourselves up. But the cares of the world were on my shoulders. I felt it was an almost sacred trust to look after my mother — my father would have expected it. Yet the thought filled me with dismay.

My sisters were not involved in this, nor did I expect them to be. Nan had a boyfriend, Harold, whom she intended to marry. Compared to Frank, he was only a boy. But he was a great comfort to her and my mother thoroughly approved of him. He was well-heeled and crazy about my sister. Nan would be making a good match, but then she never put a foot wrong. She was one of those lucky people who always knew what she wanted.

Helen was getting more beautiful every day. She was tall and slim with skin like a magnolia and big grey eyes. She was enormous fun. The world was her oyster and she knew it. She expected people to fall down and worship her as a matter of course. If they didn't, well, too bad for them. She was all go and lived life intensely. Once she stayed out all night and never revealed to anyone where she was. She went her own gay, inconsequent way without a thought for tomorrow which might never come. Perhaps it was a presentiment that she had to put a lot into a short space of time.

Our first problem was finding another house. We couldn't go on living at the Post Office indefinitely. Time was of the essence, as the powers-that-be were constantly pressing my mother to vacate the house. The great question was: did she want to go on living in Bangor? She couldn't make up her mind. Finally, Belfast was decided on. It would be to everybody's advantage and would save on train fares, an important consideration as my mother had no pension. Besides, a change would be good for everyone.

There must be some nice houses in Belfast. Nan's young man, Harold's people were in the estate agency business, the oldest in Belfast. So we thought there would be no difficulty in finding something suitable. In due course, Harold turned up with a list as long as your arm — houses for rent, for sale, small houses, medium houses, large houses, detached, semi-detached, terraced, old and new. We didn't know what we wanted, just that it had to be reasonable.

Although we started house-hunting, my mother took no interest. She wouldn't even go to look at the places we had vetted. There was something wrong with them all. But time waits for no man. We had to find some place. Finally, Frank spotted an advertisement for newly built houses in a site off the Antrim Road that seemed suitable. So Nan and I, accompanied by Harold, went to look at once. But we had looked at many unsuitable places, so had no great hope.

But the new avenue of neat little houses looked attractive. Some were already occupied and some were unfinished, but a few were in their final stages. We went on a tour of inspection.

Of course, they were very small — *bijou* is the acceptable term nowadays — and all exactly alike. But they had all mod cons, including a downstairs loo, which was very superior in those days. Otherwise, they were standard two down and three up — that meant a little sitting room, a dining room, a tiny kitchen, plus a scullery and pantry; two decent sized bedrooms and a small one. There was a small rectangular garden, front and rear. It had neat railings in front and a little gate with a minute path to the front door. There was room for a bed of flowers or something under the sitting room window.

How were we four females and all our belongings going to squeeze into such a small space? But we'd looked at other places, and the Antrim Road was best of all. My mother was persuaded to look at it and grudgingly decided that for the money it wasn't bad. But she insisted that the kitchen should be extended.

So we organised ourselves, pretty well I think, deciding what we could sell or otherwise dispose of. Some sad decisions had to be taken. Carpets were laid beforehand and curtains hung. It was not difficult to put up the beds and the bedrooms were allocated — twin for Nan and Helen, front bedroom for Mum and the little one for me. Then we placed the other bits and pieces of furniture to their best advantage. There was a boiler behind the dining room fire that provided hot water and heat. It was a complete change from Bangor and that was all to the good. But it wasn't sound-proof, and you could hear the neighbours.

26

As we gathered round the dining room table that first night in our new house, we decided it wasn't by any means perfect, but not bad.

It was a merry party. There was Helen, holding hands under the table with her young man — handsome Jack. Jack the one time, part time sailor had only scrambled into the Royal Navy at the very end of the war by lying about his age. Although now a civilian, he still retained a certain air of naval elegance and slang. He would have liked to have remained in the Navy, but it was a case of "last in, first out" and he resented that. His father's linen business did not appeal to him. Nevertheless, a handsome ring adorned Helen's left hand.

Nan was very happy too. Her future was secure with her good tempered and funny Harold, who sat beside her. Although Harold was great fun and fond of amateur theatricals, it didn't seem exciting to me. But that wasn't her aim in life. Good solid security and a place in an established society were more to her taste.

Last of all, there was Frank, so generous and kind. He had already assumed the status of the family's Head Boy, pouring the unaccustomed wine with an experienced hand. He might have had plans that at the end of the day that Mum would live with us. He was generous and also fond of her.

He raised his glass. "Here's to good luck in the Antrim Road."

We all drank the toast, even my mother, still in the solemn black she was to wear for the rest of her life.

What did she think of it all? Everybody around that table was making their own plans for the future. But what were hers without my father? She could never be really happy now. Yet there were some consolations. She approved of our young men — Frank and Harold and Jack. She was close to achieving what was then considered a maternal duty — to get her daughters married, and well married. For the moment, all was well. We'd had this wonderful family party for openers. And so to bed and the beginning of another chapter.

But all was not as it seemed. Frank had to go. I remembered my father's last command to me and couldn't lead him on any longer. So, now I was desperately planning how to give him his congé. Oh, I had no doubt of his ability and ambition, but marriage still had no place in my immediate life. And I knew he wouldn't settle for less. Before he committed himself further, I had to get the courage to bid him farewell. It was mean — he had done so much for us and I had accepted everything. Also, I'd miss his generosity. My mother probably guessed my intentions, but, to her credit, said nothing.

There was another nail in Frank's coffin. An advertisement for Kruschen Salts was beginning to appear on every available bill board. The figure advertising its alleged marvellous properties was the very image of Frank. It was silly, but I came to believe it was him. In stations, in the papers, on every bill board, everywhere I looked, I saw Frank. There he was, disporting himself like an imbecile, a grin splitting his face from ear to ear to show his large horse teeth.

Was I going mad? Maybe he wasn't the spitting image, but he seemed so to me. "There is nothing either good or bad, but thinking makes it so." To me, Kruschen Salts and Frank became synonymous. If his fate wasn't settled before, Kruschen Salts did it.

There was no confrontation. I simply accepted an invitation from another man to go to the theatre. The man meant nothing to me, but Frank saw us and never spoke to me again.

I wrote and apologised. I didn't really mean it. It wouldn't happen again.

But he never even replied.

I was cut off, as if I didn't exist. I felt very mean and small and humiliated. But, in a way, what a relief! I was free.

So we settled down to a more or less harmonious life in the Antrim Road. My mother's time was almost completely taken up with creating a garden. I think she was somewhat happy, although she must've missed Joe. He would've known how to deal with a headstrong daughter who didn't seem to know on what side her bread was buttered. But before long other chaps were knocking on the door. Still, I felt isolated and was considered an eccentric by my two sisters, who had secrets which I didn't share. I could hear them in their twin beds, laughing and talking. Two girls whose futures were settled to their entire satisfaction — or so we thought.

But nothing stays the same. The time came when Harold gave Nan an ultimatum to marry him. I don't think she wanted to be tied down to matrimony just then. We were jogging along very nicely. She didn't have any responsibilities and was being feted and wooed. I've no doubt that she was a virgin. She dictated the terms, poor Harold dangled at her heels like a well-bred puppy. Now he wanted marriage and manhood.

Harold's parents, the Russells, were very condescending. They probably paid little attention to their second son's infatuation with a girl they'd never heard of. Perhaps it had happened before. But when he told them that he'd entered into a formal engagement, from which he was not to be deterred, they must've thought it was time to give the girl the once-over. The older son, a professional soldier, was already married to a local girl. He ended up commanding the Irish Brigade.

So the day was set for Nan to meet them. Poor Nan, nervous as a kitten, put on her best dress.

"Good luck," I whispered as she left.

She arrived home, shaken but unbowed, and armed with an invitation. "They want to meet you all. Especially Mum."

Harold's family were part of the smart but stuffy Lisburn set. Lisburn was a market town settled by Huguenots where there were many linen mills. It had a completely different atmosphere to Bangor, which was a carefree seaside town with a changing population. My mother would never have moved in the Russell circle and now that my father was dead, she was poor. So she was very much on her dignity about accepting their invitation. She wrote a little note, telling them she would be delighted if they would come to tea at our house, naming the day. By inviting them, she would be in control. She was not being given the once-over and that was for sure.

The tea didn't put her out one bit. She invited the Dawsons, old friends, who were not in the poverty bracket. They had travelled extensively and were now in affluent retirement. Tea was served in the drawing room with a nervous Nan and Harold on view. Helen and I put in a late appearance.

The little drawing room looked very crowded when we arrived. But things were going to plan. Pa Russell was large and white-haired with thick lensed glasses. He was making a fuss of Mum. It transpired they came from the same part of the country, at least near enough. County Tyrone and County Fermanagh were cheek by jowl. Ma Russell was definitely a product of County Antrim — Lisburn — her speech betrayed her. I thought her quite unattractive. Later, I was to learn that she'd lost all her hair from the stress of many miscarriages. But we didn't get on from the beginning. In her eyes I was already on the shelf, although only fourteen months older than Nan. Then and thereafter, I was referred to as "your sister," or "your eldest daughter." I was nameless and of no importance. It was a new experience for me and maybe salutary. This attitude was quite without malice. At that time, as an unmarried older sister, I simply didn't count and so obligingly sank into the background while my sisters did their stuff.

The result of the visit was a dinner invitation for us. I tried to back out, but wasn't let off the hook.

"You're coming," Mum announced. "And that's that."

She was determined to be surrounded by her daughters.

On the appointed day Harold called for us in a very opulent and large car.

It was obvious Harold wanted Nan to sit with him, but he opened the door, saying, "Will you sit in the front, Mrs Breen?"

"No, I'd prefer the back." There was a twinkle in her eye as she nodded at Nan, indicating she was to sit with her young man, and got into the back. She looked so small and vulnerable there in her sombre black with a gaily dressed daughter on each side.

Nan had never properly described the house. It was larger than we expected — red brick with a short driveway to the front door. Acres of well-kept garden surrounded the house and there were garages and things in the background. Quite a place.

Mr and Mrs Russell were on the doorstep to greet us warmly. A white-capped maid hovered in the background and ushered us into the drawing room. Oh dear . . . it was one of the ugliest rooms I'd ever been in. The very best of good modern furniture, but no taste. Everything was brown and depressing, even the opulent curtains. It had the feeling of a room seldom used, except on state occasions. It wasn't used to laughter and fun and there was a sort of silence, until everyone started to speak at once.

It was a family party. Big brother was there with his new wife. She was plain-looking, but elegant and slightly super-cilious. Older than her husband, she must've thought us too young and inexperienced for serious attention. Poor Harold was treated like a child by big brother and addressed as Ba.

The white capped maid handed round drinks on a silver platter. I suppose we were all a little overawed. I was glad not to be in Nan's shoes. She was on exhibit and I resented that for her. But drink is a great loosener of tongues and it was quite a merry little party that trooped into the dining room to be unimaginatively fed on soup, roast beef and the inevitable trifle.

I resented being inspected and was thankful when it was time to go — not that anyone was paying attention to me. It would've been a good idea to have a few more men, as there was a preponderance of women. But it was family only, so it couldn't be avoided. But mother would have had more flair. She'd have invited others, family or no family.

I did not envy Nan.

Soon after that Nan said casually, "By the way, Harold and I've decided on a house."

I was genuinely shocked. "Oh, where?"

"It's in Dunmurry."

I said nothing. It surely meant they planned to marry in the near future. It was hard enough to make ends meet. How were we going to manage without Nan's contribution to the budget? Helen didn't earn very much.

But when I mentioned my worries to Mum, she dismissed me with a Micawber-like wave of the hand. "Something will turn up."

With the purchase of the house, wedding bells were sounding loud and clear. My sister had been filling up her bottom drawer since her engagement, unkown to me and luckily for her. She was a farseeing, provident soul and had acquired a nice little collection. I'd never have thought of such a thing. It would've been tempting providence. But Nan was good with clothes and knew how to make the best of herself.

The wedding date now had to be fixed, and there was a great deal of discussion about what sort of wedding Nan wanted. As I thought, she plumped for the traditional white one. Our unacknowledged relative, the Rector of St Peter's, who lived just around the corner from us, would marry her there.

I confess to taking no part in the plans. I simply didn't understand why, in the circumstances, she wanted such a display, especially with no proud father to give her away.

But Mum said wisely, "It's her show and and it's only once in a lifetime."

However, she put her foot down on the number of guests to be invited. They were to be kept to the minimum. Nan was determined that Helen and I were to be bridesmaids. Although it was a role I didn't relish, it would have been churlish to refuse.

As it was financially impossible to go to a hotel, the Dawsons insisted on my mother using their large and suitable house for the wedding. But I was still too depressed by my father's death and took no interest in any of it, not even in the choice of bridesmaid's dresses — they were very pretty, chiffon of all things, pink over blue or blue over pink. Mrs Dawson lent a beautiful Honiton lace veil and her husband undertook to give the bride away. Mum insisted on wearing her usual sombre black with not even a little bit of white lace. Nothing would alter her decision. She would mourn for the rest of her life and had to display the outward sign of her state.

So the great day came. Our little party occupied only a small portion of St Peter's. The groom and best man were in place and the ceremony began. I don't suppose it often happens that a ceremony has to be stopped because the bridesmaid is in tears. But that was what happened. Despite the music and the flowers, the pretty dresses and the beautiful bride, I couldn't help feeling sad. I just wanted my father to be there.

Back at the Dawson's house, I cheered up. It was literally a bower of flowers. The bride and bridegroom stood under a canopy of specially constructed roses. We drank our champagne in the garden where endless photographs were taken. Lunch was in the dining room which was amply big enough for a strictly family occasion. It was then that Nan distinguished herself by putting her lighted cigarette through the beautiful veil. Luckily there were such things as invisible menders, but it spoiled mother's day and everybody else's. It was a priceless veil.

A slightly inebriated little party saw the bride and groom onto the Liverpool boat en route to the Channel Islands, where they were to spend their honeymoon — no secret about that. Then Helen took off with her handsome Jack, and a reluctant best man was delegated to take an equally reluctant me home — where he was summarily dismissed. My mother was spending the night with the Dawsons. It was a relief, although I could see her typically putting on an apron to help with the chaos — although there was plenty of hired help.

Back in our little house alone, I tossed my glad rags into a wardrobe and sat down at the piano — my constant solace.

Then the doorbell rang.

Had I had second sight, I wouldn't have answered it.

It was one of the wedding guests who shall be nameless. The man was a lady killer, although I didn't know it. And so, that night I lost my virginity, almost by accident. It was a great risk and, of course, I knew nothing about contraceptives. Nobody did. Also I was scared and didn't even enjoy it. Does anyone the first time? I wondered how had my sister fared?

But the happy couple returned safely and were obviously thrilled with their new house. It was a decent size with a garden and outhouses. There was even a maid to cook. I wondered how Nan was going to put in the time with nothing to do?

But she found ways. Mum, for one, was cajoled into being a constant visitor. She usually stayed the night and came home laden with things. She got on well with Harold's parents and it was obvious she enjoyed herself — she was great fun when in the right mood. I'm sure she wondered why I hadn't done as well. But I was a non-starter in the marriage stakes.

Then Nan announced she was pregnant. She was now cherished by the two mothers and fulfilled her new role to perfection. What's more she'd out-passed her sister-in-law who showed no signs of such a miracle.

In that period it was thought immodest to flaunt your pregnancy. Like everyone, Nan took great lengths to hide her state with fashionable clothing. This greatly amused my mother who said with a laugh, "It's a lost cause, Nan."

My sister pirouetted in front of her. "Do you mean, I look pregnant?"

My mother shrugged. "Yes, but so long as you can cod yourself that's fine."

Nan went off in a huff. But in time, nothing could disguise it.

In those days mothers-to-be employed a monthly nurse — at least, those who could afford it. This nurse arrived a week or so before the confinement and remained for three weeks after the event. Then she handed over her charge to the new mother, or to an untrained nursemaid, or a combination of both. When Nurse McClure took up residence, her word was law throughout the household. She was a VIP and revelled in it. My poor sister had to endure that perpetual guardian of her lifestyle for week after week. Long healthy walks were the order of the day. Nurse never left her alone. To the disgruntlement of Harold, she even partook of the pre-dinner cocktail. There were no cosy chats after a long day at the office.

My sister and her doctor must have miscalculated, because the baby was almost a month late. Then the balloon went up and she was safely delivered of a daughter. But Nurse McClure had to fulfil her next engagement, so a new nurse appeared on the scene. Nan was now in complete control and popular because she had done what her in-laws had tried to do all their life — have a daughter.

The rejoicings were a trifle overdone. But even I, who wasn't a baby lover, had to admit this one was lovely. Her grandparents were besotted — a girl at last. Daily excursions were made to the shrine to the amusement of my mother. And the baby received the worship as to the manner born. Big grey-green eyes, so like her Aunt Helen's, would stare solemnly, then a little bored yawn would signify the audience was over. Then everyone would subside into whispers. I had my own methods of communicating, so did not like these encounters. I thought her more earthbound. Still, she was a sweetie.

About then, the weekend habit was established. Every Friday and Sunday night a little pilgrimage was made between Dunmurry and Lisburn by Harold, Nan and baby. I'm sure it was contrived by Mrs Russell — what joy to have an angel child in her own house. It let my sister off the housekeeping hook, but Harold was another matter. I feel he preferred his own house, but he was overruled and had to submit gracefully. At least, Saturday golf and bridge were introduced. But through the years, Nan would have liked to put an end to these habits.

So a pattern was established which we thought was permanent. My mother saw quite a lot of the Dunmurry household during the week. Nan and she met in Belfast for shopping, or best of all discussed and planned the all important gardens. They were happy, quiet days. Helen and I were not really involved. We had our own lives to lead and our own house to live in. Maybe we got a bit bored with a sister who did everything right, but we never put those thoughts into words.

27

It was my habit to return to Bangor at least once a month to visit my father's grave. It was quite a journey by tram and train and a long walk from Bangor station to the cemetery. It took the whole day, but I had the idea he'd be lonely, lying there all by himself. Besides, I needed him, so it was self indulgence in a way.

I would sit for hours talking to him.

One Saturday I walked to Carnalea after a bite of lunch in Bangor. It was a nice day and I longed for the sea breezes. So it was later than usual when I got home to a dismal sight. My mother and Helen were both crouched over a miserable fire, looking wretched.

"What's wrong?" I asked, worried.

They were as miserable as they looked.

I took control of the situation. "You're both going to bed!"

They protested, but I insisted.

Helen got better more quickly than my mother. In hindsight, it was the beginning of Mum's illness. It was obvious there was something seriously wrong. Her next few months were taken up with visits to specialists, always accompanied by Nan and me. She received treatments but nothing did any good. She was soon confined to bed and finally, we had to get a nurse. But she was fading away and without the will to live.

It's strange the way you kid yourself, but I never seriously thought Mum was dying. But one night, the nurse called Helen and me. We stood at the end of the bed and watched each tiny breath.

Helen whispered, "Do you think she's still breathing?"

I nodded.

But the nurse took my mother's pulse and shook her head.

Neither of us knew when she'd stopped. It was all so gentle and so final. She was still beautiful, hardly a line in her face. No wonder Joe had fallen in love with her all those years ago. I stood there, thinking of so many things. Of her Tyrone girlhood. Of her wild brothers and Brother Anthony's schoolroom. Of that thatched country house where she'd grown up and where we'd had such wonderfully happy holidays.

I don't know how we put in the rest of that night. Nan had to be told but we waited for a reasonable hour before rousing our Rector to use his telephone. We didn't have one, as they were scarce then, and having one was the exception rather than the rule. But Nan couldn't do without one, which was just as well now. Helen insisted on going over and, as she was closer to Nan, I raised no objection.

The next couple of days have faded. Harold made all the necessary arrangements and in due course a small funeral cortege set out for Bangor. Helen and I were spirited off to Nan's in-laws at Lisburn to warmth and kindness.

Being sisters, we were assigned to a double bed in a large bedroom. We weren't used to sharing a bed, but didn't grumble. We were too overwhelmed with sadness. There'd never be anyone like Mum. And what were we going to do now?

In the middle of the night I awoke. At first, I thought the bed was on fire — it seemed to be burning. But no, the heat was coming from Helen.

I touched her forehead. It was like touching a fire. "Helen, you've got a fever."

But she muttered unintelligibly and didn't seem to know me.

"Helen, it's Muriel. You know me."

But she didn't.

I was really frightened. Should I stick it out till morning

and not disturb the house? Or should a doctor be called? I had no experience and we were guests in a strange house. Helen might be all right in the morning, but she might also be dead.

At last, I went to Nan and Harold's bedroom and knocked on the door.

"What is it?" a sleepy Nan asked grumpily.

"Helen's very sick," I blurted. "You'd better come quickly."

Nan sighed. "Can't it wait till the morning?"

"I don't think so."

So Nan followed me resentfully to our bedroom. But as soon as she saw Helen, her alarm was greater than mine. "We'd better get the doctor immediately."

Helen was in a raging fever and definitely not conscious of what was going on. Then Nan's mother-in-law appeared on the scene wearing a night cap and we all got dressed.

The doctor came post haste and without a collar. Instructions were given on how to reduce the temperature. Then Helen was moved to another, more accessible room. But it took a couple of days to get her back to normal.

Helen was diagnosed as having an incurable heart disease, brought on by an infection — today, it could be cured by penicillin. When I was told, it didn't convey anything to me. But the doctors were specialists and could put a definite date on her expectation of life — it wasn't long.

Jack was devastated. And I don't know how we survived. The news was too bad to comprehend fully. We just didn't believe it. It couldn't be true. By this time Helen was back to normal and couldn't understand why she was kept in bed. In desperation we got other doctors but the diagnosis was not changed. It gradually dawned on us that Helen was going to die.

It was only four years since our father's death. This new tragedy came almost before we'd started to mourn for our mother. One thing we were glad of — Mum had died first. She wouldn't have survived the death of her "own chilo."

Mumper never made any secret of her preference for Helen. We made fun of it, but totally accepted it. There was no jealousy.

Now we had to make plans. There was no question of going back to our little house. In the end Nan and Harold made a generous offer — Helen and I were to go back to Dunmurry with them until it was all over. They had the accommodation and the space. The only condition I made was insisting on contributing to the expenses and that was accepted. It was easy enough to explain to Helen that we didn't want to go back to our own house so soon after our mother's death. So she agreed without hesitation.

To this day I can't think of that month, waiting for Helen to die. We watched her gradually get weaker and weaker. Finally, we got a nurse and she faded away like a flower, so beautiful even at the very end.

Nan and I were very close in those quiet days. And the sweet baby, as good as gold, was carried away a lot by her doting Grandmother. They would have gladly kept her altogether, she was such a happy little thing.

After Helen went, a wide empty blank faced me. Nan and Harold should have their house to themselves, so I'd no intention of staying even if asked. They now went back to Lisburn for weekends again, so I was left to myself except for their housekeeper. What would I do next? Where would I go? In my bereaved state, men didn't interest me. So I took to scribbling in a small way, a habit I've kept up all my life.

Meantime I trailed in and out of Belfast to my job. But I knew I had to make a clean break. There was no place in the present family structure for me. I was a single woman, a maiden aunt. Then, out of the blue, I heard the siren voice of London. I'd never been there before and didn't know anyone who lived there, but it beckoned irresistibly. I didn't mention my idea to anyone, fearing it would be laughed to scorn. Although we had the vote and some economic independence, the age of absolute freedom for ordinary women had not arrived. We were still tied to the family. There were exceptions, of course, but I wasn't one of them.

With these secret plans, it was a great surprise when the head of my department summoned me to his presence. He was a nice man and maybe had a soft corner in his heart for the likes of me.

"Would you like a change?" he asked simply.

I nodded. I was rarin' to go.

"Would you consider London too far away?"

I couldn't believe my ears. "You mean work in — London?"

"Yes, but would you consider it too far away from your relatives and friends?"

"No. I'd love it."

"It could probably be arranged — a vacancy has occurred. But I can only give you a short time to accept."

"I accept now!"

My answer did not leave him in any doubt. He put the pros and cons before me, reminding me that I might not get the job, but that he thought it would suit me.

I was walking on air. I just knew the job would be mine, such is the confidence of youth.

I was right. Within a week, I was given official notification to report to London as soon as possible. I was the last link Nan had with her family, so there were tears when I told her. Still, there must have been some relief.

I steadfastly refused to set foot in our Antrim Road house. I just couldn't face it. So I made over everything to Nan who would, after all, have the heartbreaking chore of sorting everything out. She agreed after persuasion. The house was to be sold and I was content with that.

The time of departure came. It was really a leap into the dark as I didn't know a soul in that vast city. Nan and Harold saw me off. There were no tears — not visible at any rate.

"Good luck," my sister whispered, kissing me goodbye.

I was on my own and stood on the deck, watching the

lovely Irish coastline recede. I was bound for a club for Professional Ladies in Vincent Square, London. Me, a professional lady? What a hoot! I started to hum,

> With a bundle on my back,
> There's no one can be bolder. . . .

Actually, I had shed a bundle of dreadfulness. Wondering whether to wander into the bar before bed, I noticed the sky was ablaze. I'd never seen anything like it. Light shimmered in many colours and I thought I saw thousands of figures, nebulous, but figures all the same. Was this the unseen cloud of witnesses we are told surround us? Was I seeing them for the first time? It was awesome, but it disappeared as quickly as it had come.

I went to bed and slept the sleep of the just.

In the morning, the stewardess brought tea. "Did you see the aurora borealis last night?" she asked, pulling the curtains. "It was glorious."

I had to laugh — so that's what she called it. But I knew differently. They were the unseen witnesses who would always be with me.